BEYOND LOSS
IN A PANDEMIC

FIND HOPE AND MOVE THROUGH GRIEF
AFTER SOMEONE CLOSE TO YOU DIES

LINDA DONOVAN

This publication is designed to educate and provide general information regarding the subject material covered. It is not intended to replace the counsel of other professional advisers such as doctors, psychologists, lawyers, or financial planners. Readers are encouraged to consult with their own advisers regarding specific situations. While the author has taken reasonable precautions in the preparation of this book and believes that the facts presented in the book are accurate, the author assumes no responsibility for errors or omissions. The author and publisher specifically disclaim any liability resulting from the use or application of the information contained in this book. The information within this book is not intended to serve as emotional or therapeutic advice related to individual situations.

The stories of people you'll read about here are composites based on real-world examples. They don't refer to any specific individuals.

Because of the dynamic nature of the internet, any web addresses or links contained in this book may have changed since publication and may no longer be valid.

Names and identifying details have been changed to protect the privacy of individuals.

Thought Leadership Success, LLC
Santa Cruz, California
lindadonovanbooks.com

Author photo by Barbara Brooks

Beyond Loss in a Pandemic: Find Hope and Move Through Grief After Someone Close to You Dies / Linda Donovan
ISBN 978-1-7379553-0-6 print
ISBN 978-1-7379553-1-3 ebook
ISBN 978-1-7379553-2-0 audiobook

Library of Congress Control Number: 2021922195

Praise for
BEYOND LOSS IN A PANDEMIC

"Linda Donovan's new book can be a valuable guide and a road map to get back on the track to surviving, adjusting, making the right decisions, and getting back into life. The author is an experienced grief support advocate and a talented writer who has walked the hard path of grief and loss herself. It certainly will be a book I will recommend in my psychiatry practice and teaching to anyone seeking information or support for painful, incapacitating grief and loss."

Ronald Parks, MPH, MD, writer, blogger, psychiatrist, and author of *COVID-19/Mental Health Crises*

"Reading *Beyond Loss in a Pandemic* is like having tea with a caring friend who provides the comfort of experience and practical tools for navigating grief and loss."

Diane Syrcle, Chief Mission Officer, Hospice of Santa Cruz County

"This book shines with practical, down-to-earth suggestions for those who are grieving the loss of loved ones during this devastating pandemic, with many stories that readers can identify with. As a psychotherapist, I've been struck with the complexities of grief that are showing up as clients struggle to rebuild their lives after all the many layered losses they've experienced in the years of the pandemic. This book will be a welcome resource for them to turn to!"

Alexandra Kennedy MA LMFT author of *Honoring Grief, Losing a Parent* **and** *The Infinite Thread: Healing Relationships Beyond Loss*

"Dealing with death is difficult in the best of circumstances. But during a pandemic? Linda Donovan gives coping techniques that are wonderfully useful, heartfelt, and wise. Arising from her personal experience as a widow and grief support volunteer, her stories ring of truth. As a recent widow myself, I find her book to be an important source of comfort and guidance."

Alesa Lightbourne, PhD,
Prize-winning author of *The Kurdish Bike*

"My father died in 2020, but not directly from Covid. The lockdown—a harsh form of solitary confinement—killed him. Struggling to get the support I needed, I found Linda's book very helpful in getting over the anger I felt over his premature death. Her clear and concise guidance gave me a roadmap for this difficult journey."

Denise P. Kalm, author, coach, blogger

"This engaging guide to loss during the pandemic era couldn't be more timely. Organized into short, easy-to-read chapters, the book is designed to appeal to the full range of those who've experienced loss, not just widows and widowers. The author offers many frank examples from her own life, and reading the volume is like chatting with an old and valued friend, just one who is wiser and more experienced than most! I particularly valued the italicized stories, which made the book's life lessons vivid and memorable. If you've experienced loss, this is a volume you'll return to time after time, as, with Donovan's counsel, you navigate the difficult path back to joy and satisfaction."

Margaret Gordon, hospice volunteer visitor

"To say this book fills a need during a pandemic is an understatement. Even without one, *Beyond Loss in a Pandemic* would still be needed because grief is universal and will have to be dealt with in order for those left behind to move on. The book recognizes that the culture has shifted post-lockdowns where people now 'appreciate small pleasures of eating at a restaurant, visiting with friends, hugging their kids.'"

Kyle Suen, web consultant

"Linda Donovan has provided a much-needed safe haven for those of us who have suffered loss and trauma from the pandemic, and beyond. Drawing on her expertise as a guide for the grief-stricken and her own journey of recovery from loss, she presents sage strategies for extricating oneself from the bleakness of tragedy and returning to a place of connection, optimism and even joy. There is a focus on the harm the pandemic has caused: the illness itself, the grief to those who could not be personally present with their loved ones in hospitals, guilt at believing they might have done more to help or even that they might in some way have infected a loved one or put them at risk, job loss, isolation, abiding fear, and more. But her gentle guidance is equally applicable to pre-pandemic trauma. Donovan's approach to healing is practical, understandable and accessible. It is something from which we all can benefit."

Karen Kaufman, Ph.D., Psychologist

I could relate to the many meaningful vignettes she presented about how other people coped with their problems. There were concrete examples about what they did to get through this difficult time of their lives. The best suggestion was to create definite objectives for what to do now and in the future. This was emotionally satisfying because they were small steps toward rebalancing my life. I strongly recommend this book to help with loss during COVID.

Margie Lafia, retired teacher

To my family with love and gratitude.
To the memory of Paul, Lenny, Lillian, Elinor,
Linda Lou, Al, Shelly, and Kelly.

CONTENTS

INTRODUCTION

The COVID-19 era is a time that so many of us would like to forget, especially when we're trying to recover from the loss of a relative, partner, friend, or colleague. I keep wishing this pandemic was just a dream that never really happened. That way, unfamiliar phrases like "shelter in place" and "maintain social distancing" didn't really exist and were merely a figment of my imagination, along with the images of overcrowded hospitals and morgues. You might feel that way too.

Consider how dramatically things have changed. In 2019, if you saw someone enter a bank wearing a mask, they'd probably get escorted out by a security guard. In many places in 2020 and even in 2021, you can't leave home without a mask. Eventually, wearing a mask indoors while shopping became second nature, like remembering to bring your keys when you're ready to take a drive. With the rapid spread of COVID variants, these mask mandates are likely to continue to change or fluctuate in some areas.

And who could have imagined that for many people, *zoom* went from being a word that describes moving quickly to a lifesaver, the Zoom software that has brought families, friends, and others together in the vastly expanding virtual world? Or that suddenly trying to find paper towels, cleaning supplies, and toilet paper in your local grocery store would become such a challenge for months on end in America? Many of us across the country experienced the shock of suddenly losing jobs, housing, or people close to us, and this has been happening while we were coping with unrelenting natural disasters and other hardships.

1

After the pandemic shutdowns began in the United States, some friends, colleagues, and family members familiar with my experience as a grief support advocate and my book *After Loss: Hope for Widows, Widowers, and Partners* asked me to update it to address the ongoing challenges in the time of COVID-19. They also wanted me to expand it to include coping with the loss of other relatives and friends. Those requests motivated me to write this book, along with the many people I knew who lost someone during this time or earlier and never got the chance to work through their grief. I set out to expand on and develop new strategies to help navigate this surreal period and the future while finding ways to feel better. Examples include:

- Learning how to stay connected with others and avoid feeling isolated, even when it might not be possible to meet in person

- Establishing certain rituals, like journaling, to express your feelings

- Discovering what help you might need and how to get it to cope with how your circumstances and role might have changed as a result of this loss

- Exploring approaches to understand and deal with any guilt or regrets you might have after losing this person

We've witnessed overflowing hospitals and long lines of jobless people parked in cars who waited for hours to get food from charities and government agencies. We're familiar with the frantic scramble and frustrations people initially experienced trying to get an appointment for a vaccine earlier in 2021. Now, at least in the United States, vaccines are more readily available to those who are eligible to receive them, although variants are causing COVID-19 surges once again and have disrupted the brief sense of normalcy we experienced as communities and businesses reopened. In some countries, COVID-19 cases are soaring, and we've seen recent rises domestically in certain areas.

While vaccines and emerging treatments offer the potential to return to many aspects of life before the pandemic, the impact of social isolation on mental health and the fear of what happens next can make the healing process more challenging. But don't let that discourage you from taking steps to work through your grief.

I realize that there's no denying the unsettling circumstances we've all experienced since the pandemic began. We're reminded of its impact each day, even as travel picks up to some destinations and businesses and schools cautiously reopen and in some cases close down again. When I walk by the shuttered restaurants and empty buildings that once held vibrant retail stores, and see more people sleeping on the sidewalk, I wish that it were only a very sad scene in a movie. It just doesn't seem real.

I'm also hopeful. After more than a year of imagining smiles underneath the masks of people as they walked on once-busy streets, life no longer seems quite as surreal. I can see some people smiling again—at least outdoors in uncrowded places. We are slowly getting back to certain aspects of life we enjoyed before the pandemic, although the impact of variants have once again demonstrated the need to proceed more cautiously. Many of us still have to work through the grief of losing someone and build a life alongside of it.

The effort to pick up the pieces can be exponentially more difficult now, whether someone you know (family, friend, or colleague) died due to COVID-19 or another cause. This struggle also applies if the loss occurred years earlier, you never dealt with it in the past, and the chaos and isolation of the pandemic were or continue to be more than you could or can handle. You may have even experienced more complicated grief with multiple losses of friends and relatives. This book is designed to offer some helpful guidance and comfort based on best practices in grief support and real-world situations.

In my previous book, *After Loss*, I shared examples of how people overcame common struggles as they adapted to their new lives and made incremental changes. If you were working through the loss of someone who died before the pandemic, the social, physical, psychological, and economic impact of COVID-19 could likely have slowed down the healing process.

You're certainly not alone. This has been an overwhelming time, but together we can persevere. I'll share with you techniques to help address obstacles and how you can once again experience joy, even in some of the simple things that we often take for granted. In fact, many people recognize how the pandemic has made them really appreciate small pleasures — like eating at a restaurant, visiting with friends, walking in a park, and hugging their kids.

Everyone experiences grief differently, but I do understand what it's like to have someone pass away during the pandemic and not be able to visit with or say goodbye to them, attend a memorial service or funeral, or even be able to comfort other family members in person after someone dies. Two of my relatives died suddenly in 2020. Additional people close to me lost family members or friends from COVID, cancer, or other causes during this period and in 2021. My heart goes out to them and to you.

When someone you love becomes seriously ill or terminal, having to suddenly become a caregiver can change your life and perspective instantly. I had no prior training in caregiving and was thrust into that role in 2005 when my late husband Paul was diagnosed with cancer and died six months later. I experienced the pain of watching him die and realized that he wouldn't be with me to witness his children grow up or ever get to meet his future grandchildren. You might have experienced this feeling as well, depending on your situation.

At that time, I was frustrated because I couldn't save him. It was a rude awakening when I finally accepted that I couldn't control his cancer. I could only control how I'd react to it. That's how practicing self-care, working or moving through your grief, and developing a support structure can make a difference. You'll learn more about that in this book.

I was fortunate because I had the benefits of great hospice care when Paul was ill, and the grief support resources improved the quality of our lives. That motivated me to become a grief support volunteer for my local hospice in 2008. I've been leading support groups for the hospice ever since—originally in person and now in virtual meetings. In fact, I was surprised and amazed at how effective these virtual group meetings were in keeping people connected, engaged, informed, and motivated—even during such an unprecedented time.

Sudden deaths can be a shock, especially because you may be unprepared for the aftermath. When I was in my thirties, my dad died of a sudden heart attack. If I possessed the experience and knowledge at that time about how to cope with grief, it would've been so much easier to deal with that horrific loss and to comfort my sons at the time, who witnessed his death. Instead, it took me many years until I finally moved to the acceptance phase of grief. I can only imagine how painful this must have been for my two sons, who loved their grandpa.

Although this book focuses on death as a loss, other circumstances have compounded the situation. The pandemic has caused severe job disruption in certain professions and industries. Just think about the parents who had to figure out how to help their kids with online school sessions while also trying to get their own work done. Add in ongoing natural disasters (fires, hurricanes, floods, heat waves, and more), social upheavals, isolation, the impact of new responsibilities, and major financial pressures, and you get multiple crises that feel like endless battering.

These converging demands can be overwhelming, particularly when you combine them with the death of someone close to you. This book explores new ways to adapt, grow, and maintain your sanity and well-being.

I've included some earlier content from *After Loss* in this book, along with new chapters and information to guide you through today's challenges. You'll discover how to stay connected, positive, and motivated—even if you have your own health issues or are recovering from the emotional and physical demands of being a caregiver.

Perhaps you have other family members or friends who are also struggling with the same loss that you're dealing with or other losses. Remember this: there's no right or wrong way to grieve. Some people might hesitate to discuss their feelings, but you can still tell that they are in pain. I'll explore what you can do to understand their issues and be supportive.

Although this book doesn't replace professional help, it's designed to provide you with comfort and resources. The stories of people you'll read about are composites based on real-world examples. They're about people dealing with many of the issues you might experience. They don't refer to any specific individuals.

Are you ready to move forward and rebuild your life as you move through your grief and work on the challenges you face? Here are some questions to help you decide. You'll find out how to address them and other circumstances in this book.

- Would you like to learn how to deal with everyday challenges?
- Are you interested in knowing more about self-care and how to make incremental adjustments that will make your life easier?
- Are you looking for ways to stay more physically and emotionally healthy?
- Would you like to find out how to cope with any lingering feelings of survivor's guilt or unfinished business?
- Do you need more insight into what you truly want now that your role, relationship, or situation has changed?
- Do you know how to get the emotional, logistical, and financial support you might need?
- Are you interested in going back to work, volunteering, or engaging in social activities but don't know how to get started?
- Would you like to learn more about how to stay connected with people and build on relationships, even when you might have more limited opportunities than before the pandemic?
- Do you need help dealing with family dynamics or changing friendships and understanding how others are affected by this loss?
- Have you thought about what it takes to declutter or simplify your home or life?

- Do you know how to set healthy boundaries with people?

- Are you struggling with deciding where to live or how to make other major changes?

- Would you like to identify and set some achievable goals that are important to your happiness and well-being?

- Have you figured out some of the best ways to avoid loneliness and isolation?

- If you've lost a husband, wife, or partner — either before the pandemic or more recently — are you interested in socializing with people? If so, do you know how to do this in a way that's comfortable for you?

Let this book be your road map for adjusting to your new life and helping you to achieve fulfillment, hope, and happiness again. I found a way forward and so can you — even during these extraordinary and challenging times.

1

REFLECTIONS
ON LOSS

It takes a lot of work to put your life back together after a loss, especially now. You may wonder why you're still feeling stuck or struggling, even if it's been a year or longer since someone close to you died. To complicate matters, depending on your relationship with that person, there could be unrelenting financial, emotional, legal, physical, and logistical obstacles to conquer. The list goes on and on. Plus, when you combine these issues with the unknowns, changes, and trauma related to the pandemic, it becomes even more overwhelming.

Here's a dramatic example of how one family was able to work through a tragic circumstance of multiple losses related to COVID.

Laurie and her husband, Tom, lived with their two young adult daughters a few blocks away from Laurie's parents. Both of Laurie's parents contracted COVID-19 a few months after it first appeared in the United States. Laurie's mother became very ill and was hospitalized. Shortly after, Laurie also caught COVID, became very ill, had pneumonia, and spent a week in the hospital, struggling to breathe.

Laurie's mother died alone in a hospital and wasn't able to have any visitors. By the time Laurie was well enough to return home, her mother had already died. Laurie knew that once she fully recovered from the virus, she'd have to look after her aging father, Sam, while consoling her two children about the loss of their grandmother.

Sam had tested positive, but fortunately never got symptoms. However, he felt incredibly guilty because his wife died, and his daughter almost didn't survive. Things took a turn for the worse a few weeks later when Laurie's husband, Tom, who was suffering from cancer, died of congestive heart failure.

This was every family's nightmare. In just a short time, Laurie lost her husband and her mother. While recovering from her own health problems, Laurie also had to look after her father and try to keep her daughters from falling apart with grief. Laurie's lifestyle was very modest. She was able to make ends meet but knew that at some point she'd have to reenter the workforce. For now, however, her focus was on the emotional, physical, and logistical challenges that she faced.

Laurie knew that contending with these multiple losses was more than she — or anyone — could handle on their own. Her local hospice, which had cared for Tom during the end stages of cancer, gave Laurie one-on-one virtual counseling sessions. In addition, the hospice team provided individual counseling for her daughters. Laurie also reached out to her pastor, who met with her virtually as she worked through multiple challenges.

There are no easy answers to coming to grips with the grief and the expanding responsibilities that Laurie never expected. However, seeking help made a big difference. Before COVID-19, it took all of her energy to run the household, care for her terminally ill husband, and provide a sense of stability for her daughters. Now she had to process the anger and sadness related to losing both her mother and her husband. She also had to face the traumatic reality that she had almost died and tackle some of the lingering consequences associated with having "long COVID."

To compound matters, Laurie never even got to have a service for Tom or her mom. Funerals and memorial services traditionally offer people a sense of support, especially when they can share good memories of the deceased and be comforted by friends and family. Laurie decided to wait until the lockdowns were lifted and hold two very small, separate outdoor services with just a few family members in attendance. Her best friend set up a web page for Tom and for Laurie's mom, and invited people to post pictures, comments, and memories.

Losing someone during the pandemic has shaken traditional ways of healing by limiting face-to-face interaction and creating more anxiety. This is where support services can make a huge difference. By limiting the scope of the memorial service, getting resources to help with her father, and seeking out spiritual and practical guidance, Laurie was able to create a path for healing.

Although I didn't experience that depth of loss during COVID-19, I can still truly empathize with people and their frustrations during these unprecedented times. I recall dropping my elderly mother off in a parking lot of a hospital for surgery at the height of the shutdowns in 2020, knowing that I couldn't even go into the building, sit in the waiting room, or see her until she was released. I understand why they had those protocols, but it was unsettling. Even before she entered the building, I'd say things like "Don't go in the elevator if anyone else is in there," worried that she might breathe someone else's toxic germs.

As the months went on, other experiences brought the reality of the COVID-19 era home. One man I know was in the hospital for months while his wife was at her senior living facility and couldn't visit him. This restriction broke her heart—literally. After her husband passed away, she became increasingly lonely, feeling like a prisoner in solitary confinement. I believe that the isolation and the rules that limited face-to-face contact with her family contributed to her heart failure shortly after her husband died.

What really shocked me, though, was when another person I know was turned away from a crowded hospital. The doctor said that she just needed to rest at home and take medicine that he prescribed. Sadly, she died suddenly about a week or so after she became ill. Her family was shaken, trying to comprehend spending their lives without her. Her husband blamed himself because he couldn't get the hospital to admit her. But it wasn't his fault. Like most of us, he did what the doctor told him to do. The hospital was filled with COVID-19 patients crammed in tight spaces where the medical staff worked nonstop trying to keep up with a steady stream of sick people.

I could go on and on about how these situations have become all too familiar. However, although it's important to recognize the depth of anguish that people are experiencing, I wrote this book to help them find that glimmer of hope and rebuild their life alongside their grief. Sometimes this transition requires slowing down enough to break away from daily distractions and identifying small goals that can be easily accomplished. Goal setting requires looking at the big picture.

That "Aha" Moment When Your Grief Shifts

Did you have any defining moments that made you think about what would help you to adapt better after losing someone? Here's when I knew it was time to break out of my comfort zone: I never lived alone until my youngest child left home to attend college several months after Paul died. It was a shock adjusting to an empty house with no one to keep me company except my Jack Russell terrier, Roxy. Since I worked from home, I spent more time with my dog than I did with people. Roxy sat at the kitchen table next to me in her chair — like a person — with her paw on the table, expecting me to give her more food.

It dawned on me that while I loved Roxy, there was something wrong with this picture. I needed more contact with people. The key was in figuring out how to get started. (Don't get me wrong. I know that animals can be a great comfort, especially for people living alone. In fact, since the pandemic began, there has been a dramatic increase in people who have been adopting pets and relying more on their four-legged friends to provide companionship and comfort.)

You might have experienced a time when your grief shifted, and you're now thinking about the next steps toward creating a more balanced and satisfying life. The approach you use may vary, based on your age, support network, economic situation, or health, and your relationship to the person who died. It can also be influenced by where you live, how the person died, any unresolved issues, and complex family/stepfamily situations. I'll show you how to take those circumstances into consideration, create a plan that works best for you, and implement it at a comfortable pace.

Although the path to rebuilding your life or simply coping with the situation until you're ready to do more may seem frustrating at times—especially now—you can emerge from this experience with resilience and insight that you never expected. You can take steps that will be comforting, practical, and rewarding over time.

Think about how this pandemic might have made you consider things that people often take for granted—like being healthy or having the freedom to go where you please. I never imagined that suddenly I wouldn't be allowed to visit with people when and where I wanted. It didn't dawn on me that there would ever be a time when I couldn't even hug or hold my new grandchild, let alone not be able to have him see my smile. This was the first time in my entire life where I saw yards of empty shelves in grocery stores. There were curfews and times when we told not to even leave our communities. On those occasions where I had to drive a long distance to help care for a relative, it wasn't easy to find an open restroom along the way or even a place to get some food. So many of us may have also missed in-person weddings, graduations, births, and other happy occasions.

The social isolation was more intense than I had ever imagined. People who were sick had to be separated from their healthy family members in their own homes, and the entire family unit had to quarantine. Families with children contended with closed schools and sitters weren't available. If the parents were fortunate enough to keep their jobs and work remotely, they also had to fill in as teachers for their kids. Currently, throughout America, many children are returning to school, yet often there are considerable restrictions in place and adjustments these students have to make.

But then I think about some glimmers of hope that can help you work through your loss. You may suddenly discover that you can really appreciate the most basic experiences you previously took for granted. When outdoor restaurants reopened in my area, having lunch out felt like being on vacation. A walk in a park can bring you closer to nature. I've even seen how people in grief support groups on Zoom have been able to establish close connections that could lead to long-term friendships. Friends have told me about the surprising healing power of virtual memorial services where relatives from all over the world have gathered and shared memories of the person who passed away—people who wouldn't have been able to attend a service during normal times because of the distance.

Keep in mind that when you lose someone close to you, your own identity changes. When your spouse or partner dies, you'll have to fill their role as well as your own. When you lose a parent, particularly your last remaining parent, you suddenly become an orphan, or orphaned adult, for the first time in your life. Losing a child or a sibling can also cause a dramatic change in your family structure and well-being.

Whether your loss includes other relatives (aunts, uncles, grandparents, cousins) or friends, there's a huge gap to fill. I'll show you how to take actions that can help you to feel better. Perhaps you'll pursue a rewarding hobby or career or take steps to be more financially secure and healthy. Or you might be able to expand your existing support network and meet new people. There are so many things you can do that will help you work through your grief and move forward.

Be open to exploring new possibilities in the future and understanding how loss can provide insight into who you are now and what you want.

2

Knowing What to Expect the First Year After Loss

There's no right or wrong way to cope with loss, especially now. In fact, you may experience many different emotions at the same time, such as sadness, anger, confusion, and guilt. Having these different emotions is normal, so go easy on yourself. You've been through a lot.

So much has changed in grief support strategies since Elisabeth Kübler-Ross explained what at the time was considered the stages of grief in her book *On Death and Dying*, published in 1969. She identified these stages as denial, anger, bargaining, depression, and acceptance.

These stages don't occur in any particular order. Not everyone experiences all of them, and sometimes people go back and forth from one stage to another. Did you know that the Kübler-Ross approach was originally designed to help dying patients and later became a model for survivors?

Over time, however, the Kübler-Ross model has changed in the grief support community to focus more on *tending* to grief. This involves working through tasks related to accepting the reality of loss, experiencing the pain, and adjusting to living without that person while still maintaining a connection with them through your memories and through others.

I'll discuss an interpretation of this new model and how it can help you in more detail throughout the book. I'll also review how the pandemic has added another layer of complexity in managing loss. You might have experienced post-traumatic stress — coping with loss compounded by the complexity, uncertainty, and isolation caused by the pandemic. The time of COVID-19 has been characterized as an ongoing traumatic event that has exacerbated the grief process and made it more complicated.

There's another type of grief that Kübler-Ross identified, known as *anticipatory grief*. If the person you lost was terminally ill or had another serious medical problem, along with COVID-19 symptoms, you may have also experienced anticipatory grief before they died.

Anticipatory grief, just like grief after loss, can cause you to be distracted and to have trouble making decisions and concentrating. You may struggle with basic tasks, experience sleeplessness, and overeat or undereat. Losing someone or watching that person decline is painful and a lot to process. I'll say this now and mention it throughout the book: go easy on yourself! It may feel like your world has turned upside down, and it takes time to put it back.

Anticipatory grief can lead to behaviors that aren't normal for you — behaviors related to grief. That's why, for many people, the mourning process begins before someone dies. For example, it may start when that person is diagnosed with a terminal illness or debilitating disease, or exhibits signs of dementia. Or if your relative or friend was taken to a hospital with COVID-19 symptoms, your grieving might have begun as soon as they were admitted.

Some people who tested positive but were asymptomatic or who had moderate symptoms had to watch others close to them struggle for many weeks before passing away. As a survivor, you may have had to grapple with anticipatory grief during this struggle. When you couple that with the fear that you might become very sick or even die as well, it's scary.

This level of anticipatory grief for others and for yourself can be traumatic. It can put you in the mode of "I'll get through each day minute-by-minute," or it can cause tremendous anxiety, depression, and mental paralysis. If this happened to you, understand that you're not alone. Anticipatory grief, combined with the fear of how COVID-19 could affect your own health and the well-being of others around you, creates a level of uncertainty and chaos along with survivor's guilt.

As you work your way through grief, particularly if you have the help of a trained professional who understands what you're dealing with, then it should become less difficult for you to adjust to the reality of the loss and its traumatic impact. Even if you can't meet in person, having a virtual meeting with a trained professional can make the difference between being able to adapt, evolve, and reengage or to remain stuck. So don't be afraid to ask for help.

Although you may be experiencing the pain of grief, you'll discover that it should diminish over time when you get the necessary help to guide you along this unwanted journey. Of course, certain triggers can cause you to temporarily move a few steps back, just as you're trying to move ahead without the person who died and find a way to maintain your memories of them. Over time, you'll learn to adapt to this loss while carrying the memory of this person in your heart.

Denial Is Normal

Grief after a loss may begin with denying the reality of death, especially if it happened suddenly. I'll review some examples to help you understand how this could be affecting you. As I mentioned, it's common to move back and forth from one emotion to another. Remind yourself that you're not going crazy. You're just grieving.

Denial helps protect you from dealing with too much grief all at once. Even if the person you are mourning had a terminal illness, and you thought you were prepared, it's still a shock when the death finally occurs. It takes time before the reality of the loss sinks in. For example, you might walk toward your dad's desk, expecting him to be there, and then realize that's just not going to happen. You may call out his name, hoping to hear him reply.

In some cases, you could feel relieved after loss if that person, such as your mom, had a debilitating illness and is no longer suffering. Still, you might have a strong desire to stay in contact with her, even though you know logically that she can't respond to you. Believe it or not, communication, even if it's just one way, can help ease the pain.

There are so many ways to communicate. Some people talk out loud to their deceased relative or friend. They know the person is physically gone and can't respond, but at least they can feel that some form of dialogue is taking place. If you don't express your emotions and say what's on your mind, then it's hard to deal with what you're holding back. I'm not advocating talking to a person no one can see when you're out in public where others can hear you—unless you're visiting a gravesite—but when you're driving in a car or at home alone, this type of dialogue can be helpful in the short term.

Here's how I dealt with this challenge. After Paul's death, I kept his cell phone line active and called it each night before I went to bed, just to listen to his voice-mail message. I could've simply kept a recording of his voice, but somehow I felt more connected to him by actually dialing his phone number. I convinced myself that if I could hear his voice, then he was still with me, even though I knew it didn't make any sense. I needed to hold on to something that was familiar until I was ready to let it go. For me, it was his voice. One night at 2:00 a.m., I dialed the wrong number, and a man answered the phone and said hello. It shook me up so much that I decided it was time to close Paul's cell phone account.

Many people struggle with sleep after loss, especially after the death of a spouse or partner. I took Paul's framed picture and placed it on the pillow where he used to sleep, and kissed it good night every evening. When my dog knocked the picture off the bed, I decided it was time to put that picture away too. That's when I decided it would be helpful to keep a journal — my nightly letter to Paul.

The process of journaling is very useful, and I recommend it, particularly if you like to express your feelings on paper. Journaling also helped me to cope with other losses. When I lost other relatives in late 2019 and 2020, I wrote them letters. Of course, I didn't mail the letters, but it felt good to write to these people and express how much they meant to me. I also shared my thoughts about them with other relatives. I describe in more detail some ideas on how to make journaling part of your routine in chapter 3. Writing frequently about your emotions, thoughts, and questions is an approach to help you work through the denial phase more easily.

But writing is just one of many ways to express your feelings. Some people have also built altars in their homes or gardens as a place to "communicate with" and honor the dead. Others have created artwork, written songs, or expressed their feelings through cooking. I know a woman who makes an apple pie every year on her late son's birthday in his honor. She doesn't even eat it, but cooking is her way of showing her love and sharing the pie with other people who know her son.

It's likely that some of your friends, who may not have experienced loss, don't always "get it." They may seem to be judgmental because they don't understand how these ways of connecting with your deceased friend or family member can be helpful and normal. Don't let these concerns discourage you from finding techniques to help you cope. Do what makes you feel the most comfortable and let others know that how you decide to grieve is your own choice. It's not their fault, but they can't always put themselves in your shoes.

Denial and shock are common emotions when someone dies unexpectedly, such as from a sudden heart attack, accident, or COVID-19. People who watched someone suffer through a sudden death might have the added burden of helplessness and sometimes survivor's guilt. They were present when it occurred, yet were unable to prevent this tragedy from happening.

It's also traumatic if someone died and you were the first person to find them. It takes time and effort to finally release shocking images from your memory and to stop tormenting yourself with the "what if" questions. These can include haunting yourself with questions like "What if I called the doctor sooner? What if I forced the ambulance to take my dad to the hospital instead of trying to treat his condition at home because the hospital was overcrowded? What if I was home when this happened and was able to prevent this accident?"

You don't have a crystal ball. You can't see the future. Please, don't blame yourself for something that's beyond your control. Instead, you can work on releasing those feelings. By focusing on the positive memories of the person who died, the traumatic and heartbreaking images can dissipate over time, and they may eventually disappear entirely.

If you've had to cope with a suicide, murder, or accident that you weren't able to prevent, the emotional loss is particularly devastating. You could be suffering from post-traumatic stress and not realize it. So the denial phase may last even longer than you'd expect. Don't forget that help and support can be available to you. Grief support from a hospice organization can be very helpful, particularly beginning with one-on-one support before deciding whether you're ready to join a grief group. You also could greatly benefit by getting help from therapists, psychiatrists, and religious leaders. The trauma can be intense, and it may require multiple levels of support.

Experiencing Anger

Anger is a common reaction to the pain of grief and shows its face in many ways. It's okay to be angry. You just lost someone important in your life. It hurts, it's unfair, and you could also be scared. You may be angry at the doctors for not saving your loved one's life or angry at yourself for not being able to change the outcome. You may also be angry at the person because they died and left you alone at a time when you really needed them.

If your dad died of COVID-19, you could be angry at family members or whoever you thought might have caused the illness, even if everyone was careful. Or if you survived and your wife didn't, you might blame yourself—even though it's not your fault. Remember, the coronavirus is an invisible enemy. You couldn't have seen this coming.

If you weren't able to have the type of service that provides people comfort during normal times, that's another reason to be especially angry. The isolation, fear, and confusion during the time of COVID-19 caused people so much pain as deaths were mounting. People in need of medical attention for other reasons were also under extreme stress and haven't always been able to get the support they required. Supplies have often been limited, and staff members are frequently overworked. Many lives were lost because people had to postpone medical procedures or were afraid to get treated when the virus surged in their areas. Hospitals were overcrowded. Morgues were jam-packed with long waiting lists.

You have every right to be angry and sad. In fact, as this book is being written, some countries are under siege by the variants and are experiencing growth in daily cases. In the United States, the delta variant has caused hospitalizations to reach new pandemic highs for people under fifty. Intensive care units in parts of the United States had started to fill up again. Hopefully, the pandemic will subside dramatically as more vaccines, treatments, and other resources become available to people who need them.

We often blame ourselves for not doing enough when someone close to us dies, even when we tried our best. When Paul died of cancer, I blamed myself for not having greater control over his diet. I thought that I should have tried harder to convince him to follow a healthier diet and go light on the ice cream, cheese, and bread.

I couldn't let go of my feelings of guilt until a grief counselor gave me some sage advice: "He's an adult, and it was his choice to eat those types of foods. Plus, it's also unlikely that this diet caused his cancer." After hearing her reassuring words, I gave myself permission to stop being angry about something that was out of my control and probably would not have made a difference.

Some people are upset at themselves because they weren't home when their friend or relative died. Instead, they may have found that person passed out on the floor, and it was too late to save them. A common reaction is, "If only I had gotten home ten minutes earlier, I could have called an ambulance, and she'd be alive today."

Or you may have been present during the death and hopelessly watched as someone had a heart attack. Even though you called 911 immediately and attempted CPR, there was nothing else that could have changed the outcome. Or you could be angry at yourself for postponing the trips you wanted to take with them, or other activities you put on hold.

It's normal to be angry. You may be angry at your deceased mom, for example, for giving you COVID-19 (even though you survived and recovered) and for not taking better care of herself. You may feel that she somehow unwittingly contributed to her own death and your illness. Perhaps your relative, partner, or friend, after refusing to take the medication that the doctor recommended, died. Or that person didn't follow the CDC guidelines and continued to hang out in bars and other crowded places at a time when it wasn't considered safe. You may be angry that they didn't listen to the doctor. Conversely, if the doctor couldn't save them, you might be angry at the doctor—even though the doctor tried to do everything in her power to help.

We've experienced how communications and actions related to controlling the pandemic have kept changing, as doctors, scientists, and the CDC learned more about the disease. Physicians had to delay certain exams and tests and were forced to stop some surgical procedures or accept other patients because hospitals were overcrowded with COVID-19 patients. When this happens, and you lose someone, it can make you angry at an unresponsive system that didn't protect the person you cared so much about.

One woman I know whose husband died from cancer in early 2021 had to contact twelve different morgues the day he died trying to find a service provider available to take his body out of her house. There were so many coronavirus-related deaths at that time in her community that the morgues were overflowing. Imagine her frustration and anguish as she had to come to terms with the loss of her husband while finding it nearly impossible to get the help that is normally available at such a traumatic time!

When someone close to you dies, you may feel abandoned, yet you still have to deal with the complexities associated with loss. It's not unusual to be angry at the world and blame yourself, doctors, your spouse, a higher power, others, and the lifestyle choices of the person who died. While it's normal to feel this anger, there are ways to release it.

Coping with Guilt and Regrets

Feeling guilty and having regrets can happen before and after a loss. As I mentioned earlier, this is where the if-only and what-if statements are common. You may try unsuccessfully and illogically to bargain with a higher power, by saying out loud, "What if I give up ten years of my life so that my husband can live?" You may explore hypothetical situations, for example, "I'll do anything, God, if you can just make my child live again." This is what Kübler-Ross called bargaining.

After the person dies, you may torment yourself by thinking about what you would do differently if you could simply change the past. It's where you might say:

- "If only I had taken him to another doctor and gotten better advice sooner, he might have lived."
- "If only I had been home when she had a heart attack, I could have saved her."
- "If only I had taken him to a different hospital when he was turned away because it was overcrowded."
- "If only I didn't visit my grandpa and unwittingly give him COVID-19, he might still be alive."

Sadly, people can spend years punishing themselves for not recognizing the signs of someone's illnesses or failing to understand that certain situations were out of their control or totally intentional. They might ask themselves:

- "Why can't I have another chance with him?"
- "Why did I let her stay in a job that was stressful and that might have contributed to her heart attack?
- Why did I survive the car accident and my child didn't?
- Why am I okay but my wife died of COVID-19?
- Why did I let my son join the military and put himself in danger?

You may carry guilt and regrets with you, and that's common. We tend to take responsibility for things that aren't our fault. Yet the loss must be dealt with and worked through. Sometimes there are no explanations that make sense. After all, you can't see the future, and you can't change the past.

Bad things happen to good people. Accidents and unfortunate situations occur. Illnesses are simply part of life. All you can do is focus on where you are now and determine how to learn from, cope with, or make positive changes as a result of this loss.

Here are a few examples of how I transformed the insight I gained from Paul's illness and death into new, positive experiences.

Long before Paul and I knew that he had cancer, we wanted to travel, but we kept putting off the trip. Usually, our work schedules got in the way. Then we had unexpected bills that made it seem impractical to spend the money. There were always excuses to avoid traveling. I shared with my friends details about the vacations that we had planned but never took and how sad I was that I missed these opportunities. After listening to me, one couple immediately began saving for vacations, and now they regularly take trips together, based on my suggestions.

I traveled overseas with our girls a year after Paul's death. Whenever possible, I also tried to slow down (at least a little), become more flexible, and savor precious moments with my family and friends. When my first grandchild was born, I made myself available for babysitting whenever I was given that opportunity, no matter how busy my work schedule was at the time. I would fly or drive to visit people important to me whenever possible before the pandemic. Since then, I've made what seems like endless hours of driving to stay connected, and it's worth the effort. That's a lesson that grief teaches people. You only have so many days on this planet, so make the most of them.

Many people are starting to do some of the things that gave them pleasure before COVID-19 and make up for lost time to get back to some of their pre-pandemic routines. Even if you're not in a position to travel, emotionally, physically, or financially, there are still ways to maximize the value of each day. If possible, get outside and enjoy spending time in a park, field, beach, lake, desert, city, or whatever place that makes you feel more comfortable.

Perhaps you don't feel like going anywhere but want to relax. Maybe you just need to simply pick up the phone and call a friend or post a positive message or inspiring picture on social media. Making time to take a warm bath, watch your favorite show on TV, play an instrument, listen to music, or have a friend stop by for a visit (even if you only feel comfortable meeting outdoors) are simple ways to make your day special.

Coping with Feelings of Anxiety, Loneliness, and Depression

You have every right to feel sad, lonely, anxious, and depressed when you lose someone. You're not alone. The most optimistic people can also experience these emotions after loss. It's overwhelming and a lot to process, especially early on.

What do these emotions look like? Mealtimes, which were once an opportunity to connect with the person you are grieving, may no longer be enjoyable. Your own eating habits might change.

Looking forward to the daily routines of breakfast, lunch, and dinner may fade when that person is no longer there to join you. Some people simply cut back on food. After all, if the relative or friend had lived with you, and now you're the only one at home, there's less incentive to cook for just one person. Others compensate by overindulging in food or alcohol. Doing activities alone or without that special person, like going to a special restaurant, movie, sporting event, or play—activities that you may have enjoyed doing with them—can be potentially stressful and lonely until you're ready to experience them again.

I've known some people who rarely left their houses months after losing a child or partner, even when they were invited to gatherings by well-meaning friends. Instead, they withdrew from engaging in outside experiences to the point that going to the grocery store made them anxious.

When you're grieving, it can be challenging to make decisions. You could have trouble deciding whether you should read the newspaper or let it remain on the kitchen table. You may leave weeks of mail or email unopened because it's just more than you can handle. Or, if you open the mail, you might find an unexpected bill that you're not prepared to deal with at the time, and it can add to your stress level. You could fail to listen to or answer telephone calls because this requires too much emotional effort, and you don't feel like explaining yourself to anyone. You have limited resources, grief can sap your energy, and so some of these behaviors that seem unusual to you are really normal reactions.

Although I think it's important to connect with people, sometimes you might not want to engage with others until you're ready. Even phone conversations can be overwhelming when you don't know how to respond when people ask you how you're doing. If you tell them you're not fine, they might ask probing questions that you don't want to answer. Consider sending a text or email, thank them for their concern, and tell them you'll get back to them at another time.

The simple act of taking a shower and changing out of your bathrobe, pajamas, or sweats can be a chore that you might put off for a few days. That's why trying to establish some sort of routine—"I will get out of my pajamas and dressed no later than 10:30 a.m." — can be helpful. I must confess, however, that even though I'm not grieving now, there are days when I find myself skipping that important routine. I just have to remember to make sure that the camera on my computer is turned off!

Getting back to the topic of overload and grief, when my father died unexpectedly of a heart attack many years ago, I looked at a pile of laundry a week later and thought, *How am I ever going to be able to wash this?* That was so unlike me at the time — I had always been proud about the ability to multitask my way through life. (That was the old me. I work at a saner pace now.) So why did performing a simple, daily task like laundry suddenly seem so difficult? It was because I was unknowingly working my way through feelings of depression, trying to adapt to a world without him, and was overwhelmed. The most basic chore seemed daunting at the time.

As the loss settles in, your emotions might vary. You may cry suddenly without knowing why. (That's why we have tissue boxes on hand at every grief support group meeting.) Perhaps even more unsettling is *not* being able to cry because you're so sad that you can't release the pain.

If you were a caregiver for the person who died, you were probably running on adrenaline for a long time and putting your own needs on hold. Taking care of your wife, for example, may have been your full-time job. When she died, your job as a caregiver was over. All of a sudden — particularly if you have retired, have your own health issues, or don't have much of a support network or other major responsibilities — you may feel extremely isolated and bereft.

If you were or are a caregiver during COVID-19, the stress is exponentially greater because of the trauma caused by isolation you might have experienced, lack of or reduction in medical support available, and the fear of becoming ill yourself. The job of being a caregiver kept you going, but it took a physical and emotional toll on you, which is often referred to as *caregiver fatigue*. That's why it's so important to give yourself permission to spend the time necessary to take good care of yourself, especially after loss.

Adjusting to the Change in Your Life

There *is* light at the end of the tunnel, although it may be awhile before you see it. Acceptance is where you finally come to terms with the fact that this person is not physically coming back and your relationship with others might also change. This perspective helps pave the way for adjusting to a world without them. If the person you are grieving lived with you and died in your home, you might look in the closet and see that his clothes are still there. Her picture may still be on the wall. His files and books may be scattered about the house, but the only place you'll actually see him is in your dreams.

Dreams can be comforting and help you through this transition period, although not everyone dreams about the deceased person. Perhaps you're in too much emotional pain to have these dreams, but if you can remember them, dreams can help you to sort out your unconscious emotions. Think about keeping a dream journal by your bed and jot down your dreams as soon as you wake up. See if you can find meaning in any patterns.

Paul died fifteen years ago, and I still have dreams about him. In them, he's returned, and I try to explain to him about all the changes in technology that he missed because he died in 2006. One of my favorite dreams is seeing him ring the doorbell, and I shout, "You're back! You're not going to believe all the things you can do with the iPhone today!" Then I show him

32

how he can use it to take pictures or videos, do FaceTime calls, and so much more. Of course, once I woke up, I realized that it was just another dream, but the dream actually brought a smile to my face.

Sometimes I've had dreams where he's always in his late thirties, even though he died at fifty-seven. It's common to remember people when they were at their peak and not at the age of their death.

Getting back to the discussion around the acceptance phase, by accepting the loss, you may begin to understand that you'll have to deal with the change that has been forced on you. Over time, you may be prepared to take mini-steps and set incremental goals, particularly if this person played a key role in your life. At some point, you could be able to visualize where you want to be over the next few years — or just the next year — and focus on your most critical priorities. Ultimately, when you come to terms with the fact that this person had died, you can identify the actions to take to find happiness and fulfillment again.

Some people set goals and then a timetable on how to reach them. For example, if you relocated temporarily to move in with your mom to help take care of her before she passed, perhaps your goal might be to sell her house and move to a place where you'd be most comfortable. If you intend to move in another year, then you can start to schedule what needs to be done to get her house in shape and ready to put on the market and how long it will take to put your life back together alongside your grief.

Other people can't seem to reach a level of acceptance in what can be considered a reasonable amount of time. Before COVID-19, getting through the first year after loss was often the biggest hurdle. However, the pandemic introduced so many additional challenges that people haven't had to deal with in our lifetime. That's why it can take longer to reach a point of acceptance and adjustment. Don't get discouraged.

Some examples below show how people dealt with loss before the pandemic, and other examples are directly related to how people adjusted during the COVID-19 era. Regardless of when these losses happened, these stories demonstrate how loss affects individuals and ways to cope.

Mark was unjustly irate at the staff members who cared for his wife at a nursing home and blamed them for her death. He spent many years being angry and researched ways to sue them. Although he never took legal action against the facility, his anger continued to build. He wasn't able to see that the staff did everything possible to keep his wife, Bella, comfortable and alive. The facility had an excellent rating, and the staff members were attentive to Bella. Sadly, Mark couldn't accept the reality that Bella died because her heart was weak and eventually gave out.

For twenty years, he lived with this anger. It continued to be part of Mark's conversations with his friends, who became weary of hearing the same old story repeatedly. Because Mark couldn't accept the circumstances of her death, it sapped a lot of his energy and held him back from experiencing or enjoying new opportunities that became available to him.

The bottom line: if you want to avoid Mark's fate, try to accept and release the pain associated with what can't be changed. If you can't do this on your own, consider getting therapy, grief support, or both. Many people also find comfort by reaching out for help through their local place of worship.

At the other extreme is Nia, who accepted a loss more quickly and also used what she learned from this experience as a way to assist others.

Nia got to know the people at the nursing home who took care of Ben, her partner. A few weeks after Ben passed away, Nia wrote a letter to the director of the facility, thanking the staff for keeping Ben as comfortable as possible. Nia accepted that Ben's time was limited due to his severe illness.

About two years later, Nia volunteered to teach a knitting class at the facility in appreciation of the staff's efforts to care for Ben. She was able to manage her grief in a positive manner, come to terms with it, and feel good about helping others at the same time.

Some people accept the loss, adjust to accommodate it, and then return to feeling depressed, angry, sad, and guilty. Remember that with grief, you may take two steps forward and one step back. Set realistic expectations, but be patient with yourself when you backslide. You've been through a lot. Expect some relapses. This is normal.

Gabriel's ten-year-old son, Julio, died of cancer after a yearlong battle. Gabriel's wife, Ariana, quit her job to care for Julio and couldn't make herself go back after his death. Ariana stopped contacting her friends and became increasingly isolated. Gabriel and Ariana were so devastated as their son

*became increasingly ill that they barely spoke to each other —
even during the times they couldn't leave the house due to
COVID-19 lockdowns.*

*When Gabriel returned to work, he tried to hide his grief from
his friends and co-workers. Whenever anyone asked how he
was doing, he responded abruptly with, "I'm fine" and then
quickly changed the subject.*

*It became clear that they were both depressed and in need of
some guidance. Gabriel, who previously had been just a social
drinker, increasingly turned to alcohol for comfort. Ariana,
however, slept. And slept. And slept. That was her coping
mechanism. By sleeping throughout the day, she could avoid
thinking about Julio. The house that was once orderly was a
mess, with dirty dishes piled in the sink, paperwork strewn
throughout, and huge stacks of laundry waiting to be washed.*

*When Angela, Gabriel's mother, would visit them, she became
aware of the changes in her son and daughter-in-law and
encouraged them to get help. At first, they didn't listen. It took
several months before Angela could finally persuade them.
The couple met with a hospice grief counselor virtually and
got additional help from their church and other community
resources. Eventually, they were able to recognize that the
habits they had formed as a result of their grief were making
it much more difficult to put their lives back together and reengage with people, their jobs, and life.*

Some of your friends may feel awkward talking about loss, and
they may unknowingly say things that can be hurtful. They

might not understand what you're dealing with and expect you to bounce back quickly. Their comments are not meant to hurt you. They just might lack your perspective.

People who haven't lost someone close to them don't always understand that grief comes in waves. They may not realize how disturbing it is to hear someone say, "It has been many months since he died. I thought you'd be done grieving by now." Be open with your friends and kindly ask them to refrain from judging you. Let them know that you are still working through your grief and that you're moving at your own pace.

This same advice applies when communicating with people who don't understand the impact of a miscarriage. They may think that you can recover much faster than if you lost someone who had been in your life for a long time. But that's not a fair assumption. They don't know the depth of your loss.

Adele was four months pregnant with a daughter when she had a miscarriage during the pandemic. She and her husband avoided talking about the baby after the miscarriage and continued to keep busy. It would've been their first child, and she had been looking forward to being a mother her entire life. People told her they were sorry, expressed their concerns, but they treated it as lightly as if she just got over having the flu.

Adele became increasingly anxious and lost interest in exercise and other activities that had once been enjoyable. She and her husband, Dmitri, grew more distant. She blamed herself for the loss, even though she followed a healthy diet and took extra care while she was pregnant. Her friend Brianna suggested that Adele see a therapist to help her work through the trauma of losing the baby.

37

The therapist helped Adele to realize that it wasn't her fault and that she should take the time to mourn this loss, even though it was early in the pregnancy. Adele gave the baby a name, Amelia, and started to journal about her feelings. Adele realized that she had to recognize and acknowledge this as a loss, and share her feelings with Dmitri. They decided to wait another year and try again for another child. In the meantime, by talking about their feelings instead of hiding them, Amelia and Dmitri became closer once again.

It can be somewhat easier to adjust to loss after you get through the first year because you'll know that you made it through those difficult milestones — birthdays, anniversaries, and holidays. For some people, though, the first year is such a blur that the reality of the loss doesn't sink in until later, especially since the pandemic has been such a disruptive force. They do their grief work in the second year and beyond.

The COVID-19 era has exacerbated this situation because of everything that people have had to put on hold. The extended time of social isolation made it difficult to get the same level of support and comfort from friends, family, and the community pre-pandemic. Exercise classes at health clubs that had provided an opportunity for people to take a break, stay in shape, and congregate were off limits. They have opened up again in some places.

Yet many people are holding off returning to the health clubs because of concerns about being exposed to COVID-19 — even if they're fully vaccinated. At this time, there are still some unknowns about the virus and variants, causing some people to delay returning to the health clubs that were able to survive the shutdowns. Others are returning to these facilities but are either avoiding going during peak hours, exercising outside, or changing their routines.

Imagine how college students who lost a friend or relative must feel during this time. In addition to the loss of someone close to them, these students might have had to give up a year, or more, of the in-person college education they had expected. They may have needed to spend a year basically isolated in their apartments without too many options to leave, participate in group activities, or even see close friends or family members. They lost someone, and more than a year of their lives was disrupted. They never have imagined a pandemic would happen—not in their lifetimes. But it did.

And it wasn't until April 2021 that vaccines started to become available to them in the United States, along with improved treatments for those who have caught COVID-19. It will take time to adjust to the pain they weren't able to address when so many support groups weren't available for in-person meetings. It's important to help these students feel good about any of their achievements or positive activities—no matter how small—as they begin to work through their loss and process it.

Your friends and family members may be reluctant to talk about the person who died because they don't know how this conversation could affect you. They may not realize that part of working through grief involves sharing stories and happy moments. They don't understand that talking about what made your partner, relative, or friend so wonderful can help you on your path to healing.

By sharing your experiences about the person who died, the good memories will come to the surface. Eventually, the traumatic images of watching a loved one slowly deteriorate from cancer or another type of debilitating condition will fade.

Over time, those images are often replaced with the memories of when the person was vibrant and healthy.

I no longer remember what Paul looked like when he was dying and had lost sixty pounds in a very short time. When I think of him, the only image that comes to mind is that of a healthy, happy man.

Common Reactions to Grief

When you're grieving, you may experience different emotions at once and be easily distracted. Your social interactions with others might change. You may find yourself talking out loud to the person you lost and be more likely to question and worry about your own mortality.

How do you determine if some of the problems stem from grief, stress, or other challenges that you are facing? I often share the following resource with people in grief groups and with friends who are grieving to give them insight into what's happening to them. It's from "The Journey of Grief," by Hospice of Santa Cruz County. The information in the chart helps people to realize that the emotions they are experiencing, along with the changes in how they interact with people and their environment, are totally normal. Look closely and see how this relates to your experience.

Physically, you may experience:	Many different emotions can be felt at once:	Your thoughts may include:
Exhaustion	Sadness	Disbelief
Emptiness in stomach	Loneliness	Distraction
Tightness in chest	Anger	Absentmindedness
Shortness of breath	Guilt	Forgetfulness
Dry mouth	Anxiety	Dreaming of him or her
Increased noise sensitivity	Shock	Poor concentration
Appetite changes	Relief	Memories of other losses
Sleep disturbances	Numbness	Denial
Low motivation	Depression	Diminished self-concern
	Sudden crying	
	Fear	
	Helplessness	
Socially, you may feel:	**Your actions may include:**	**Spiritual questions may come up:**
A need to withdraw	Carrying special objects	What will happen to me when I die?
Less desire to converse	Crying	Where is my loved one or friend now?
A need to take care of others	Visiting the gravesite	How could God allow this?
	Talking to the person who died	When will I die?

Source: "Journey of Grief," Hospice of Santa Cruz County

Common Grief Reactions

Look at the chart on page 41 whenever you have doubts about why you might be distracted or why your reactions to people and situations are much different than before you were faced with the loss. It will help you to realize that what you're experiencing may be due to grief. Many of these emotions and reactions will diminish over time. Since traditional forms of support might not have been available to you during the time of COVID-19, and because the impact of the pandemic likely intensified the loss, give yourself extra time to heal.

Dealing with Multiple Losses

Multiple losses compound and create complex grief. As I've said, the losses we all experienced during the COVID-19 era make this exponentially more challenging. If you haven't fully worked through prior losses of friends and family members who have passed, then it will be much more difficult to manage the one you are dealing with now. It's common for people to avoid mourning, but you can only put it off for a while. It's the work that you have to do.

I attended a workshop where Alexandra Kennedy, a licensed marriage and family therapist and author, discussed the concept of creating a grief timeline, which can help you to understand how the death of important people in your life has affected you. She also discusses a timeline in detail in her books, *Honoring Grief* and *The Infinite Thread: Healing Relationships Beyond Loss*.

Sample Grief Timeline

Reconstructing a timeline gives you the opportunity to explore how you reacted to those losses. I'll use my own family as an example to help you prepare your own.

- Early 1960s: One of my younger cousins died of leukemia. I was just a child, and we got a phone call that he was gone. There was no fanfare. One day he was here; the next day he was not. I missed him and never fully understood the impact of this loss until much later in life.

- Mid-1960s: My grandparents on my father's side both died about a week apart. No one talked about my grandparents except to say they were gone. I was sad, but there wasn't really any closure. I was just told that they were old and sick and that their deaths were to be expected.

- Mid-1970s: My grandfather on my mother's side died of a heart attack. By then, I was an adult and had gotten to know him. I saw him in the hospital before he died and got to say goodbye. For the first time in my family, death wasn't glossed over. I attended his funeral and had a few dreams about him after his passing.

- Early 1980s: My grandmother on my mother's side died of a heart attack, and this death really hit me hard. I was very close to her, saw her frequently, and recently had made plans to go out to lunch with her the week of her death. I had dreams about her for several months after her death and thought about her often. I never got therapy or grief support for the loss. I just kept on going.

- Late 1980s: One of the worst days of my life occurred when my fifty-seven-year-old father died of a sudden

43

heart attack while on vacation with my mom and my two boys. It was such a shock. Although I was married and had a wonderful husband and family, I had no idea how I would cope with the loss of my father. I somehow managed to keep myself together to help organize his service and deliver the eulogy. I never went to grief counseling or had therapy at the time. I just assumed that when someone dies, you have to be brave and move on quickly. For many years, I tried to connect with him in my dreams. I thought about him at night and imagined that he was still present and guiding me in my thoughts. It was very hard to accept his death. I was so focused on my own loss of my father that I didn't even realize what my mother or sons were going through.

My sons had to witness their grandpa dying in front of them. Along with my mom, they experienced not being able to do anything to save him. None of us got grief support or therapy, which could have made it easier to adjust to this loss. Instead, my family and I just threw ourselves into activities so that we didn't have to face or deal with the pain.

My mom and I were both workaholics, so we just loaded up on projects and stayed busy. I told my sons that it was very sad that their grandfather died, but we didn't talk about it much. In retrospect, I realize that I didn't get the support needed to understand how this loss could have affected them and others.

- Late 1990s: My father-in-law, Paul's dad, died after a long illness. I was prepared for his death because we knew he had been sick, but of course I was saddened by the loss. We had closure with a funeral and the support of family members. I worried about the impact this had on Paul's mom, Paul, his brothers, and other family members.

- 2006: Paul was diagnosed with cancer in November 2005 and died in less than six months. This time, I was better prepared than when I lost my father. With the help of hospice, a social worker was available to address my anticipatory grief issues as Paul's health became progressively worse. After his death, I attended one-on-one sessions and a grief group. Our daughters got counseling. When Paul died, I became more aware of the grief process and began to understand how the loss of my father and others had affected my life.

- 2018: My mom had remarried more than ten years after my dad passed away, and her husband, my stepfather, died suddenly in the hospital. It was a shock, and I was saddened. Because I understood the grief process by that time, I was able to console his children, my mom, and other family members.

- 2019: My uncle fell and died from complications of the fall. I was in frequent contact with him over the years and even edited his memoirs into a book, which he had worked on for months. By sharing his stories and staying connected with his family, I was grateful for the time I had spent with him and had closure. Still, it was eerie, yet also comforting, when I attended his funeral and saw his gravestone next to that of my grandparents, another uncle, and my younger cousin who had died many years ago.

- 2020: I lost Paul's mom, who was like a mother to me. I couldn't travel to see her because of COVID-19 lockdowns. Late in the year, one of my sisters-in-law died very quickly after she became ill. I was angry and sad. All I could do was try to stay calm, console other family members, listen to them, and find ways to provide comfort at such a crazy time. In addition to relatives, other people whom I knew either closely or indirectly passed away — some from COVID-19 and others from different causes.

- 2021: The husbands of some of my close friends died. Although their deaths weren't due to COVID-19, I felt considerable sadness for the ordeals they went through — trying to care for their husbands yet not being able to visit them in the hospital, worry about being exposed to COVID-19 (pre-vaccine), and struggling to find people who could help give necessary support at a time when COVID-19 death rates were skyrocketing.

Developing a loss timeline helped me to realize that if I could get through one loss, I could deal with another. But it also made me aware that if I didn't take the time to fully mourn a previous death, then dealing with a current one would be more challenging. This process also reinforces why it's important to get help. If you lost someone in 2019 or even earlier, and you anticipated being able to physically attend an in-person meeting with a grief support group or therapist, that option was not likely to be available to you once the lockdowns started in 2020.

Virtual support sessions have been valuable and provide people in some locations access to help they would not be able to get in their own communities. However, many people want and appreciate the advantages of a face-to-face experience. That's especially true if you're tired of spending so much time on the computer or if you live alone. The physical isolation that so many of us experienced in 2020 (and many are still feeling in 2021) further compounded and prolonged our grief.

The timeline described in this exercise refers to losing someone by death. If you add in other losses, like financial troubles, having to cope with fires or other natural disasters, losing a job, or having your own serious health issue, it can deepen your grief. If you're far enough along that you feel comfortable developing your own timeline, then give it a try, based on the directions below. If it is too painful or emotionally difficult to do this right now, skip this step. Consider trying this again in six months or so but only if you feel that you're ready.

How to Create a Grief Timeline

1. List the key losses you've had over time and how you handled them.
2. Then identify any loss where you didn't take the time needed to mourn and work through it.
3. Determine what you'd do differently, based on what you know now.
4. If you have any prior losses that are unresolved and interfering with your ability to deal with this one, determine what you can do to help release those feelings. For example, if your mother died within a short time after you lost your best friend, think about how to apply some of the principles in this book to help you have the emotional space to cope.

You'll be surprised at what you'll learn when you complete a timeline and see how prior losses are affecting you. By understanding the grief process and common reactions to it, you can get a better perspective on what's causing you the most pain and how to soothe it.

Getting By

As you move through the first year, the reality of your loss begins to sink in, although don't be surprised if this slow struggle continues beyond Year One. After all, your world might have been turned upside down in so many ways during the pandemic, and it also takes time to recognize that your friend or relative is gone. The first few months or even longer may be a blur. You might sometimes think of this as just a bad dream and hope that the deceased person will appear next to you when you wake up.

Sorting through their possessions can be so emotionally draining, and you may even put it off for many months. If you lost a spouse or partner, you might look at other couples and think, *Why do they get to have a partner, and I don't?* The same concept applies to people who have siblings and both parents. You might think, *Why do they get to have a brother or mother?*

Don't try to tackle too many tasks at once. You not only miss this person, but in some cases, you may also have to take care of the responsibilities they handled, which adds to your workload and stress. As a result, you may discover in the first few months that you can accomplish only about half or less of what you usually can do.

When friends or family members offer to help with things like chores, errands, and meals, take them up on their offers. Don't feel that you need to reciprocate right now. Consider having someone be with you as you sort through your friend's or relative's belongings or to move them to a place where you can go through them later, like in a garage. Make sure to ask for help. You know what you need the most. They don't.

If people want to bring you meals, let them. If they invite you to dinner at their homes, please attend, if you're ready. If you're too tired to walk your dog, let the kids in your neighborhood do this for you. People want to help, and these are some of the ways they can make your life easier. Don't feel compelled to write thank-you notes, either. This isn't a time when people expect you to make any extra effort. So just call or text them with a note of appreciation when it's most comfortable for you.

Accept that it's normal to want to connect with and hear from the person who died. Do whatever makes you feel comfortable. I've discussed how journaling is a good way to express your feelings and can help you transition to the changes that you're experiencing as a result of this loss. Some people write in a journal for months, while others may take much longer. Eventually, you may decide to jot down thoughts only when the mood strikes you. If that's the case, keep a notebook by the bed or someplace where you can always find it.

Many people find comfort in going through photo albums or old letters or watching videos of the person who died whenever they feel a strong need for that connection. I watched videos of Paul and my father periodically over the first few years after their deaths. Sometimes they made me feel better, but many times they would also cause me to cry. That's okay too. You have a good reason to cry, and crying releases pain.

Maintaining sensible eating patterns is a big challenge to people after loss. One widow I know ate only one meal a day for many months, except when she was with other people. This disrupted her well-being, and she became lethargic, irritable, and weak. It wasn't until her doctor warned her of the dangers of not maintaining a healthy diet that she began to eat regular meals and regain her health.

At the other end of the spectrum, a widower who had always been at an ideal weight started gorging on junk food as a form of self-medication. It wasn't until his children commented on his sudden weight gain that he decided to take dieting and exercising seriously. Losing someone takes a physical toll on your body, so do what you can to create healthy habits. Sleeping is particularly difficult for many people after loss, so make sure that you get enough sleep.

Jill rarely fell asleep before 3:00 a.m. because she felt too sad to go to bed without her husband. So she watched TV, including the news and murder mysteries, and spent evenings on her computer, long after she should have gone to sleep. Jill wound up sleeping late each morning and was out of sync with the schedules of her friends, family, and part-time work obligations.

Eventually, Jill was advised by her doctor to take a mild sleeping pill for a short period of time until she was able to maintain normal sleeping habits and change her evening routine. After several months, she was able to make adjustments that made it easier for her to sleep at night without taking a sleeping pill. She reduced her caffeine consumption to just one cup of coffee in the morning, exercised daily, and read a magazine, book, or sections from the Bible before going to bed.

Consider watching something on TV other than the news if you have trouble sleeping. Newscasts are frequently filled with negative information — who got killed in an accident or murder, how politics can disrupt your life, the many ways natural disasters are causing people to lose their homes, the number of people who died that day due to COVID-19, and so on.

Don't get me wrong; I think it's important to know what's going on in your community and the world. Watching the news late at night and listening to the problems in the world can be troubling. If you watch TV before going to bed, make it a practice to view something humorous or light. Otherwise, the negativity can seep into your dreams.

Having a positive, calming routine makes it easier to sleep. Think about the approaches people take to get a baby to sleep. I'll bet it doesn't include shouting matches on TV and stories about disasters. Instead, this might include turning down lights, listening to soothing music, and simply relaxing. There are a variety of apps you can download on your phone to help you relax before going to bed. Some of the apps have natural sounds, white noise, and sleep-tracking software so that you can look at sleep patterns. Other apps offer guided meditations.

Even the most well-organized person will probably notice the struggle it takes to stay on top of things at a time when their loss is overwhelming. There are so many things to be done at a time when you're still grieving—papers to fill out, accounts to sort through, people to contact, and decisions to make.

The amount of work is so overwhelming that you might not even know where to begin. You may want to make radical changes in your life, like moving, or immediately selling your parent's house or your own, only to find yourself making impulsive decisions. Instead, consider putting off making major decisions until a later date. Whenever possible, please give yourself time to understand how grief is affecting your reasoning before you make any big moves. Talk to people about the proposed plan. Let them challenge you. It might be the right time, but check it out first. Otherwise, you might regret a life-changing choice done at a time when you were most vulnerable and not in a position to think about it objectively.

Stephen's father died in 2019 before the pandemic hit, and Stephen inherited enough money to help put his daughter through college in a few years and cover any emergencies, such as losing a job for a period of time.

This was the first time Stephen was able to experience what it was like to live beyond paycheck-to-paycheck as an adult. He thought about ways to get rich quick. Stephen noticed how some of his friends were making money as landlords. Impulsively, within two weeks after receiving the funds, he used the entire inheritance to buy a small condo that he could rent out. He had assumed that he could just sit back and collect rent. It seemed like a no-brainer.

Just a few months after he bought the condo, his renter decided to move out and the rental market tanked. The condo was vacant for many months, and Stephen could no longer afford to pay the mortgage on his house and the rental condo. He sold the rental at a loss. As a result, most of the inheritance was gone.

A financial adviser once told me that statistically the average person who inherits a lump sum will spend it all in five years. That's what happened to Stephen. Buying a rental unit might have seemed like a good decision in the long term under certain conditions. But Stephen didn't take the time to evaluate whether he was ready to make the investment and what he would do if the rental market shifted. He was grieving. He wanted to do something to feel better and take control at that moment. In Stephen's case, it was an impulsive decision to buy a condo. And it cost him his inheritance.

At the other end of the spectrum, some people who are grieving might avoid making any decisions about even the most basic tasks because it's too difficult to consider one more responsibility or change. Getting stuck can also be a problem because certain things can't be delayed. You might have car or home insurance policies that need to be paid, even if just looking at them seems overwhelming now. If you don't have the mental energy to research whether these policies are right for you, consider renewing them and then looking at other options when you have the time and are able to evaluate them. Prioritization is critical.

If you have real problems making decisions—which is natural because your life has been turned upside down—consider hiring an expert to help you if you are able to afford it. Or think about discussing your concerns with friends whose opinions you value. They might be able to help by providing an objective opinion. Here's an example of how to create new opportunities.

After Ginny's daughter died from a childhood disease, Ginny wasn't sure whether she wanted to return to work. The loss was so overwhelming, and Ginny wasn't ready to face the demands of her job as a marketing manager. She felt burned out at work even before the ordeal of her daughter's illness. Ginny always enjoyed working in her garden and had dreamed of turning that passion into a career, but never gave herself permission to make that happen. After losing her daughter, she thought, "Life is short, so why am I wasting my time doing something I don't enjoy?"

Ginny's good friend, Tyler, would often share with Ginny how much he loved his landscaping business and working outside in the fresh air. After much deliberation about what to do with her job – should she stay, or should she go? – she decided to rethink her career.

Before Ginny had to return to work (she took a leave when her daughter was sick), she had a long discussion with Tyler about what it would take to work in his industry, the benefits and challenges, and how to get started. After meeting with him and doing more research, Ginny finally decided. She had saved enough that she could afford to make less money, work part-time for a while, and enroll in landscaping courses at a university. It took Ginny many months to make that decision, but ultimately, it was the right move.

Focusing on Priorities and Goals

Getting organized can help you focus on what's important after loss. You may have your own approach to getting started. For some reason, whenever I experience any type of loss (not necessarily related to the death of someone), one of the first things I do is reorganize my tiny clothes closet and desk. For years, I couldn't understand why I would do this, but I've finally figured it out. My closets and desk tend to be a bit unkempt. (I still have a note from my second-grade teacher that said, "Linda is a good student, but she keeps her desk messy." Nothing much has changed since that time.) Organizing the closet gives me a sense of control and a fresh start.

Before you begin looking at developing priorities and goals, pick something easy that needs to be done so that you can feel a sense of accomplishment. It might be as simple as paying bills, cleaning out your email inbox, pulling weeds in the garden, or fixing something that's broken. Then you can feel ready to move on to bigger challenges.

What are some approaches to taking control when you feel overwhelmed?

- Make a list of your top priorities and goals. Think about what you want to accomplish in the next twelve months and how you plan to get there. This involves understanding your big-picture goals and then setting incremental ones for each month. You can always work on longer-range goals later.
- Or, if thinking twelve months in advance is overwhelming, then just do a quarterly plan. And if that's still too challenging, try a thirty-day plan or even a weekly one.

Use a day planner (or a calendar on your smartphone or computer) and update it periodically with the things you want to accomplish and dates to get them done. Each night before you go to bed, review what you plan to do the next day. You may modify the list, but this approach gives you the opportunity to chart your progress and hold yourself accountable. Be your own boss.

Here are examples of priorities and goals to consider for the first year after loss.

- Stay mentally and physically healthy.
- Visit with friends and family more often. Make a few new friends.
- Take control of finances and develop a financial plan.
- Don't accept more work than you can handle.
- Invest time in a hobby or sport.

- Identify what makes you happy, gives you something to look forward to, and gives you hope.
- Travel with a friend, partner, or relative, even if that includes simple outdoor day trips.

Here are examples of goals for a particular month and how to break them down.

- See your doctor for a checkup and get on a regular eating schedule.
- Go through your loved one's closet and give away some items to friends and charities.
- Seek professional help to deal with loss, either a therapist or grief counseling from hospice.
- Exercise three times a week.
- Visit with a friend at least once a week.
- Organize paperwork and automate payments for bills.
- Plan a trip—even if the trip won't happen for many months.
- Investigate taking some classes.

Here are some of the types of items that you can add to your daily checklist. Don't try to add too many tasks in a single day. Keep the list manageable. Depending on where you are in your grief, you may only be ready to do a few daily activities initially. Over time, you should be in a position to think further ahead.

- Make an appointment to see your doctor.
- Take a yoga class (even if it's a virtual course).
- Review bill payments.
- Have lunch with a friend.
- Buy groceries.

Here's something to think about as you plan for each day. Use your cellphone to set alerts and remind you of certain events. Some people I know set timers on their phones to remind them when it's time to take their medicines. When you're grieving, it's easy to forget things, so a timer can be helpful.

If you have a job, then you may need to remove a few things from the daily list and move them to the weekend, such as the bill payments, lunches with friends, and other activities. Your daily checklist would then be something simple, like "go to work, make an appointment to see a doctor, and schedule a yoga class for one night and this weekend."

Goal setting is so important, whether you have lost someone, are working, or are retired. If you haven't identified your priorities and a path for achieving them, each day can run into the next and leave you feeling like you haven't accomplished anything. That emotion can trigger a cycle of hopelessness. Even if you only get through one or two items on your daily list, congratulate yourself for what you were able to achieve instead of feeling badly about what didn't get done.

Taking Care of Your Health

When Paul died, I knew that I had to do whatever I could to stay healthy, not just for myself but also for my family. Like many caregivers, I put my own checkups on hold because I didn't have time to visit a doctor. On a subconscious level, I didn't want to find out if I had any health problems because I wasn't in a position to deal with any other information that could be unpleasant. I was a procrastinator.

My focus had been on getting through each day and making sure I did whatever was needed to help Paul. His illness took a physical toll on me. My hair started falling out in clumps due to the stress. My eating habits were irregular. I wasn't getting enough sleep.

After he died, I got back into exercising regularly. I tried to eat three balanced meals a day, even when I didn't feel like eating. I finally did the necessary follow-up visits with doctors. Death makes you realize how fleeting life is. When you make your health a priority, you can be better prepared to handle whatever other challenges and opportunities come your way.

However, as I fast-forward to look at the COVID-19 era, I also put off routine in-person medical visits, eliminated all trips to the dentist, and scaled down my exercise routine a bit because my health club was closed. Probably many of you experienced this as well. Now I'm fully vaccinated and playing catch-up in those areas. Soon, I'll even get to hear that familiar but annoying sound of the dentist's drill once again.

Looking for Ways to Cope

Losing someone can affect you physically, just like it affected me. You may feel weak or tired. Stomach problems and headaches from the stress of loss are common. Perhaps you put off seeing a doctor for your own health matters while taking care of your friend or relative, and now you dread having to visit a doctor for yourself. Going to a medical office can bring back painful memories of the place that took care of your friend or relative before that person died. If you have any concerns, enlist a friend or family member to be with you at your medical appointments.

After the first few months following the death of someone close to you, the outpouring of help from people may subside. Then you're left to deal with the aftermath on your own. People who haven't been through your type of loss don't always realize how difficult this is for you. You will likely eventually learn how to adapt over time and avoid letting comments from others cause you additional pain.

Marge, a widow, was invited to attend the wedding anniversary of good friends shortly after the death of her husband. She was seated at a table of married people. When the music started, and everyone else got up to dance, Marge realized that she was alone. This made her feel sad and frightened. Marge also wasn't invited to dinner events with friends that she used to visit with when she was married. It dawned on Marge that she was being pushed into a world of singles, and she needed to accept her new status. She expanded her social network and developed new friends who were single.

Dealing with holidays, anniversaries, and birthdays, which were once so joyous before loss, can turn into scary events, unless you're prepared. When you have a Plan B, and you get through the first year, you're more likely to adjust better to these celebrations in the future. But dealing with these emotional triggers can often be a challenge. Think about what would make you most comfortable during these times and make plans that will help you. This can include taking the following actions:

- Surround yourself with supportive family members and/or friends during holidays and special events.
- Change your traditional holiday experiences by visiting new places, lightening your burden if you normally do the hosting, or volunteering to help out with a local charity or your place of worship.

- Have a birthday party honoring the person who died.

- If you lost your spouse or partner, be with a friend or family members on your wedding anniversary or perform a ritual that will give you comfort, such as taking a walk along his favorite hiking trail, watching her favorite TV show, or preparing a special meal.

- If you lost a parent, plan to do something with a friend that will help you get through Mother's Day or Father's Day.

As you go through the year, periodically look at your priorities and goals and see how well you've done. You may need to make some adjustments and possibly remove some things off the list if your goals were too ambitious. I always mention to the people who attend grief groups, including virtual sessions, that they should be proud that they found the courage to show up each week and share their stories and grief with the group. It's a big commitment to say, "I want some help and I'm willing to make the effort to attend."

If you lost a spouse or partner, when you went from *we* to *me*, your social circle likely changed. If you made a few new friends, give yourself credit for taking the initiative and reaching out.

Perhaps you had many sleepless nights after the loss and ate at irregular times. If, by the end of the year, you're able to sleep much better and have established a structure for healthy eating and sleeping habits, congratulate yourself for taking those important steps.

I was surprised to find that many women of the Silent Generation—parents of the Baby Boomers—found themselves paying bills and making important financial decisions for the first time in their lives after their loss. It was a big leap for some women in their eighties and beyond, who had been homemakers their entire lives, to suddenly learn how to take on new responsibilities and adapt to technology.

Keep in mind that some of these people grew up listening to the radio because televisions hadn't been sold to the public until 1939, yet they may have had to adjust to electronic bill paying, sending emails, and making online purchases. Perhaps their vision has deteriorated, and they need extra assistance. One wrong click and they could inadvertently sign up for something they didn't want. While Zoom has been a real lifeline for many seniors, others have felt left out because of challenges with the technology.

I encourage these people to get outside technical help whenever necessary. They may get this assistance from their grandkids. My own grandkids have taught me things about downloading apps that I wasn't even aware of, and I consider myself tech-savvy! You can also generally opt out and get physical bills mailed to you if you prefer.

Similarly, I noticed that some of the older men of the Silent Generation might need to learn how to make their own meals and do laundry. They also may have struggled with technology, but perhaps their wives or partners had mastered how to use a computer. These newly widowed men also had to learn new skills or get outside help. Fortunately, there are all kinds of great classes in person and online to help people learn the things they want or need to learn.

Looking Ahead as We Move Through Loss and the Pandemic

What changes can you expect by the end of the first year after loss, or even longer due to the pandemic? Change happens incrementally, and each step, although sometimes painful, puts you closer to healing.

Some people in the grief groups I worked with prior to the pandemic and those who lost someone in the COVID-19 era — depending on their situations — became more comfortable socializing in new groups. Others got closer to their old friends and family, but also reached out to meet new people.

Although it can be more challenging to make new friends as we age, don't give up. Some people have met new friends in their virtual grief support groups and have continued those friendships after the groups ended. A year after loss, you can expect to have encountered various roadblocks. The added chaos and uncertainty of the pandemic causes healing to be more difficult. However, you can expect to gradually make some inroads into dealing with the realities of your loss.

Each day, try to find something that gives you a sense of gratitude, even if it's something as simple as walking outside and enjoying the sunshine, talking to a friend on the phone, or having a pleasant meal. Try to do something that makes you happy.

Some people find it helpful to recite daily affirmations each morning. These are positive, motivational statements to set the tone for the remainder of the day. Or you can pick a few affirmations and repeat them out loud in front of a mirror several times a day to address any negative thoughts that are presently dragging you down. Here are some affirmations to consider saying:

- I'm enthusiastic about life.
- I try to live each day to the fullest.
- Even if a situation is difficult, I'll approach it with confidence and find a way to address it.

- People tell me that I'm interesting.
- I am grateful for my friendships.
- I find joy in some of the simplest things in life.
- I appreciate my friends, family, and life.
- I am open-minded and willing to learn new things.

There are also many books available with motivational affirmations if you need additional guidance to help motivate you.

3

WORKING THROUGH THE GRIEF PROCESS

How many times have you heard someone ask, "When are you going to stop grieving?" It's a common, unsettling statement. People who say this don't even realize that working through grief is a process, and it takes time to adapt. If you start crying when you hear a song because it reminds you of someone you lost, or you are uncomfortable in social situations where everyone else seems happy or coupled (if you lost a spouse or partner), you're not alone in feeling this way.

Perhaps you can't even go back to restaurants where you had meals with that special person. This reaction is perfectly normal. If you cry at your son's wedding, your daughter's graduation, or your grandson's birth because your husband, wife, partner, parent, sibling, or close friend is no longer there to enjoy it, understand that this type of response is common. Lots of people cry at these events for a variety of reasons.

Paying attention to your loss and tending to it is often known as "doing grief work." And it is work! No one grieves in the same way as anyone else; there's no one-size-fits-all template. Fortunately, you can use a variety of strategies to help ease the pain and enable you to move forward with your life. In this chapter, I'll discuss some of them and give you "tools" for moving at the pace that works best for you.

The Healing Power of Journaling

Even if your friend or relative was terminally ill and you expected the death, it's still a difficult adjustment. This can happen early after a loss, over many months, or much longer. Journaling can help you to communicate and sort through and explore what's going on in your mind.

Journaling was an easy practice for me to follow and maintain. I journaled periodically after my father died more than thirty years ago, but didn't stick with it long enough to fully address my feelings of loss and helpless. When Paul died, however, I would write down my thoughts each night for the first few months. Paul had cancer that spread to his liver and passed away almost six months after he was diagnosed. Initially, I set aside a certain time each night that was exclusively devoted to journaling. I continued to write in my journal on an occasional basis more than a year after his passing.

Although I didn't realize it, that initial routine helped me to handle daily responsibilities more effectively because it gave me the opportunity to focus on grief outside my working hours. I was working full time and taking care of my teenage daughter when Paul died. Journaling was my private time to communicate with Paul and reflect on how I was going to manage my life without him.

If you haven't tried journaling, even if it's a year or more since you lost someone, get a notebook and set aside time as needed to write about what you want to express. Or if you prefer to write using a computer, that will work too. When you see those words in an entry, they will help you sort through your emotions. You'll be surprised how this simple exercise can provide insight to guide you.

Each night at 10:30, before I went to sleep, I would write a letter to Paul and describe my day and emotions. I'd go through the usual conversations that I might have had with him if he had been alive. At times, my letters were very sad. I'd ask him questions like, "Why did you have to die so soon?"

I'd describe the day's events, whether it involved telling him about how I tackled a project at work or how the Boston Red Sox had done that day. He was a big Red Sox fan, and one of the last things he said to me while he was still able to speak was, "Did the Red Sox win the big game?" Even when they lost, I would tell him the Red Sox were doing fine. After all, why upset a dying man who has worshipped his favorite team his entire life?

One benefit of journaling is that it gives you the opportunity to ask that special person any questions that you didn't ask during their lifetime. This helps you cope with what's referred to as unfinished business.

Also, if you have any regrets, you can share them in your journal. If you regret that you didn't do enough to prevent the death (even if there was nothing you could have done), go ahead and write about it. It's a chance for you to get your feelings out of your head. Then these words no longer will be in the back of your mind when you're supposed to be mentally present somewhere else. You're essentially freeing up space in your brain, like offloading memory to a flash drive, so that you can focus on moving forward.

You might ask, "What good is journaling if the communication is only one way?" Here's why it's so important: you can actually get answers to your questions. That's right—the next part of journaling is to put yourself in that person's shoes and see how he or she would respond. Here's what a typical letter to the person who died might look like.

Jim,

I'm sorry that I couldn't do anything to stop you from having a heart attack. I called 911, but you died before the paramedics arrived at the hospital. If only I'd been in the garage when you were there and had the attack, I could have saved you. But how was I to know you were in danger? I feel so guilty, and I miss you more than you'll ever know. I can't stop thinking that if I had put my book down and checked on you in the garage before this happened, you'd be here today. I feel like it's all my fault. How will I ever get through this nightmare?

Maria

Now, it's time for Maria to dig deep down into her memory and write a new letter, this time from Jim's perspective:

Maria,

Sometimes things happen that are well beyond our control. You had no reason to believe that I was having a heart attack. Everything occurred so quickly. In fact, I didn't know I was experiencing a heart attack either. There wasn't anything that you or anyone could have done to help me.

I love you so much and want you to know how happy I was to have spent my life with you. I want the best for you. Please enjoy each moment for me, and know that I will always be with you in your memories.

Love, Jim

Think about the value of this exercise. Things that you wish could be said are expressed. By writing in Jim's voice, Maria was able to put her mind at ease with the comforting thoughts that he would convey to her. As a result, she was able to stop replaying in her mind the nightmare of that awful evening.

My initial entries in my journal contained messages of despair. Gradually, they became more conversational, to the point where I described what was happening in politics, how I managed to fix a broken washing machine all by myself, and how our favorite TV series ended. Eventually, I cut back on journaling as I became more focused on the world around me and the tasks needed to rebuild my life.

Communicate in Other Ways

I'm a writer, so it's quite natural that writing would work well for me. However, if you don't like to write in a journal, consider other ways to express your feelings. Some people routinely talk to their deceased relatives or friends out loud and then think about how that person would respond. Others convey their feelings through prayer or meditation.

Many people enjoy creating artwork to release their emotions. For example, painting a picture, building something with clay, or making a collage are practical ways to get in touch with your emotions around grief. There's also something special about using your hands to produce artwork. A friend of mine communicated her anger about cancer by throwing paint against a canvas to create an image that portrayed a tumor out of control. She even won an award for the painting, which ultimately was displayed in an art gallery.

One woman I know wrote songs for her husband and played them on her guitar. Another woman planted a garden in her partner's honor and went there daily to mentally connect with him and discuss what was on her mind. Some people play videos of the person they're grieving and then talk to them as if they were still in the room. Putting together photos or collages of that special person can be very healing. Be open to trying something new.

You never know how you're going to react to a video of the person you lost. At times it may make you smile. On other occasions, you might find yourself in tears. Still, these videos can be comforting. I recently converted some old family videos into digital files. This has given me the opportunity to share those memories with other family members. My grandchildren and others got a chance to see relatives who passed away before they were born or when they were very young.

If you're having problems making decisions, particularly those that you made with your friend, relative, or partner, ask yourself, *What would that person want me to do in this situation?* Ask your questions at the end of the day when you're less likely to encounter distractions. Then let the answers come to you.

It was just before Christmas when Denise's daughter, Elaine, who had a new baby, split up with her husband. Elaine's husband demanded that she return the wedding ring he'd given her. Denise, who had lost her own husband five years earlier, was worried that Elaine would be distraught over the breakup. At the same time, Denise wondered what she could do to make Elaine feel better.

Denise shouted out loud to her departed husband. "Sam, I need you to tell me how to help Elaine. What can I do?" She sat patiently waiting for some guidance and looked at her hands, and the answer became clear. The wedding ring that Sam (Elaine's father) had given to Denise had been moved to her middle finger years ago. The ring obviously held sentimental value to Denise, which is why she continued to wear it, but not on her wedding finger. Yet it occurred to her that Elaine really needed the ring. Denise felt that she was guided by Sam to give the ring to Elaine, which she did. Elaine proudly wore the ring in memory of her father, and it helped cheer her up at a difficult time.

Here's another example of someone who called on the memory of his father to make a major decision.

Duane had broken up with his live-in girlfriend, Ellen, just before the pandemic hit, because she wanted him to leave college, get a full-time job, and get married. Duane just wasn't ready and began to doubt whether their relationship was strong enough to move to the next level. After they split up, Duane moved back home to live with his dad to save money. In the meantime, Duane's father, Bob, tested positive for COVID-19, got pneumonia, was hospitalized during the peak of the early outbreaks, and ultimately died. Duane tested positive, too, but he didn't have any symptoms.

After Bob died, Duane blamed himself because he felt that he must have given his dad COVID-19. He started drinking heavily and sleeping throughout the day. He was barely keeping up with his classes and was unmotivated to continue with school. That voice in his head kept repeating, "If only I didn't move in with my dad, he might still be alive. I was selfish. I ended the relationship with Ellen because all I cared about was myself. If I had somehow managed to stay with her, perhaps my dad would be with me now."

The isolation of the pandemic, and the loss of his dad, was more than Duane thought he could handle. His grades were suffering, he got tired of taking classes on Zoom, and he was ready to drop out of college. When Duane visited with his uncle Bernie, he opened up and described how his life was unraveling. Bernie asked him one simple question, "What would Bob want you to do?"

Duane thought about how Bob had encouraged him to go to college, pursue a degree in a field that he enjoyed, and explained the value of finishing what you started. He shared that with Bernie, who asked him another question, "What would Bob say to you if you told him you felt guilty about giving him COVID?

Once again, Duane tried to think about how Bob would re-act. Bob was a loving, considerate father who always wanted the best for his son. Duane realized that Bob wouldn't want him to be burdened with guilt. He'd want Duane to make the most out of his life and be happy. He'd tell Duane that it wasn't his fault.

After thinking about how Bob would react, Duane joined a support group and once again began to concentrate on his courses and future career. It took time, but Duane was able to stop blaming himself for what happened to his father.

Focus on Self-Care

We put a lot of emphasis on self-care in the grief groups—encouraging you to do something that makes you happy, being gentle with yourself, limiting the number of decisions you make at a given time, maintaining a regular schedule, and so on.

Keeping a mood diary is different from journaling, and it's easy to do. Use this diary to identify what causes you stress or pain and what helps you to feel comfortable. If you can find and track what triggers certain moods, you can create a plan to provide better self-care. Here's how to get started.

1. Keep a notebook, and have each page in the notebook represent a day. I like to use a paper notebook and carry it around with me, but if you're more comfortable jotting this down on your smartphone, use that.

2. Each day, when you experience something uncomfortable, write it down. It doesn't have to be long. It could be a short sentence.

3. Also write down what made you happy.

4. At the end of the day, write down any insights this process has given you.

Here's what a mood diary entry might look like for one day.

- I called Susan, and it was frustrating talking with her. She expects more of me than I can give. This made me sad and angry.
- I took a walk and enjoyed looking at the trees in the park.
- The man who was supposed to fix my dishwasher never showed up. It got me really upset. I have enough problems without people flaking out on me.
- I liked watching my favorite show on TV.
- Insight: I'll contact Susan less frequently because it gets me upset when I have to deal with her. She's a relative, and I know she means well, but I don't have the energy to spend much time with her right now. I'll plan to walk more often in the park. I'll call someone else to fix the dishwasher when I have time. I'll watch my favorite TV show when it's convenient and I need a break.

It's amazing what you'll learn when you start tracking patterns that lead to ups and downs. If you didn't keep a mood diary, you might not realize how to cope with the impact that Susan has on you, or how walking and watching your favorite show provides a break to help deal with stress. After keeping a diary for about a month, you should have a good idea of what can help positively affect your moods, and make changes that lead to feeling better.

If you don't have time to keep a formal mood diary, then just jot down notes on a small sticky pad. List what happened, how it made you feel, and the date. Put that note on a large piece of paper. Look at the sticky-pad notes after a week or so, and see if there are common patterns in what makes you happy or sad. Then do something about it.

Coping with Unfinished Business

It's common to feel tremendous guilt about what you did or didn't do to help your relative or friend. There might be something you wanted to tell that person but never had the chance. You might also be angry at others. Writing a letter to deal with this unfinished business can be useful and liberating. It's also a way to forgive yourself, the deceased person, and whoever else you think might have contributed to the loss.

Set aside about thirty minutes or more of quiet, uninterrupted time in a peaceful setting to collect your thoughts. Complete these sentences to help articulate what's on your mind.

Message to your deceased relative or friend:

1. I love or like you because . . .
2. I'm angry at you because . . .
3. I forgive you because . . .
4. One thing I would like to say that I never got to tell you is . . .
5. If I could change anything I've said or done, it would be . . .

Message to yourself:

1. I feel guilty because . . .
2. I forgive myself because . . .
3. I'm angry at others because . . .
4. I forgive those people because . . .

The following example can help you to understand how to write this letter.

Debbie was devastated because her partner, Pat, died in a car accident on the way to the grocery store late at night. Pat had decided to pick up dessert for the two of them. Debbie had told Pat not to go to the store because it was late, raining hard, the streets were flooded, and Pat had drunk a few glasses of wine earlier in the evening. Pat was determined and decided to go anyway. On his way to the store, the road visibility was poor, and Pat crashed his car into a tree. He was rushed to hospital, but despite efforts by doctors and nurses, Pat's injuries were too extensive. He died.

Writing the letter wasn't easy. Still, it was important for Debbie to express her emotions because it was becoming increasingly difficult to concentrate and stay in the present moment. When she watched TV, her mind would wander and repeat everything that had happened on that horrible night and how the accident could have been prevented. As a result, she was unable to remember much about the TV programs she saw.

The same thoughts about that night kept jumping into her head when she'd have conversations with friends and would lose track of what they were saying. When Debbie ate meals, she was so stressed that she stopped enjoying the taste of her favorite foods. Here's what her letter to Pat looked like.

I love you because we shared a wonderful life together and have so many great memories. We raised a family, traveled the world, laughed at each other's jokes, and encouraged each other to be successful in our careers. We had many friends and enjoyed simple pleasures, like walking through the woods, reading the newspaper together while having breakfast, and watching our children grow up to be independent. We had such fascinating conversations that I always thought of you as the most interesting man in the world.

Our holidays were very special. Every Mother's Day you got up at 6:00 a.m. to put the turkey in the oven and make it just perfect so that our family could enjoy a wonderful feast. You took care of me when I was sick and put our family needs first. Your hugs and kisses were loving, and I treasured them just as I cherished you.

I'm angry at you because I told you not to leave that night. I urged you to stay in, especially since you drank a few glasses of wine, and the weather was so bad. But you didn't listen to me. Getting dessert was more important to you than your life! Now I'm here alone, and I feel like you abandoned me. I can't bear to be without you. Yet you were so stubborn that you didn't do what I asked. If only you had listened to me, you'd still be here!

I forgive you because you had no idea that going to the grocery store would lead to this tragedy. It was wrong for you to drive after having two glasses of wine, but the alcohol didn't seem to have affected you. Besides, we had the drinks three hours before you left. When they did a blood-alcohol test on you at the hospital, the results showed it was at a safe level.

The police report indicated that anyone driving in that area at night during such a bad storm likely would have experienced the same deadly outcome.

If there's one thing I would like to say that I never got to tell you, it would be that I'm sorry for all the times I complained about petty things you did that sometimes annoyed me. I wish I had been more understanding because I miss you so much, and I now think of your quirks as endearing.

If I could change anything I've said or done, it would be to have spent more time with you and worked less. I can't get that time back now that you're gone.

And here's what Debbie's letter to herself looked like.

I feel guilty because I didn't try harder to prevent you from leaving. If only I had given you an ultimatum and been more forceful in stopping you from going to the store. While I didn't want you to go, I also wanted the dessert. So I feel like it's my fault.

I forgive myself because I didn't know you would get into an accident. You'd driven to that store hundreds of times. It was only two miles away. Sometimes things are out of our control. The accident happened, and it's not my fault.

I'm angry at others because the city should've had more lights on the street. It was dark. The doctors and nurses should've done something more to save you. I don't know what it is that could've made a difference, but I'm mad that they were unable to prevent your death. I'm mad at God for letting this happen. You were only fifty years old and didn't deserve this. All of our life plans have been disrupted. How could God let this happen?

I forgive everyone I just blamed because many roads are dimly lit. It's not the city's fault. I read the medical reports and talked with the doctors and nurses. They truly tried their best. Their job is to save lives. As far as God goes, sometimes bad things happen, and there's no way to explain it. But if I stay angry, it's going to drain me. There's nothing I can do to change what happened, so I'll just have to accept it and stop being obsessed with negative thoughts.

Writing this letter helped Debbie to release her feelings of guilt, cope with unfinished business, forgive others, and set herself free.

Many religions help people cope with loss and other personal challenges by reinforcing the power of forgiveness. When you can understand what's making you angry and forgive the people and circumstances that you think may have contributed to these negative emotions, you can free up energy. Then you can make room for resilience, strength, and the desire to pursue what makes you happy. By communicating anything you would've liked to have shared with that person, you're helping to resolve any unfinished business.

Consider Grief Support and Therapy

When you lose a relative, partner, or close friend, your social circle may change. If you were in a relationship, expect that to change somewhat if most of your friends are couples.

I lived in a suburban community, and nearly all my friends were married. It has now been about fifteen years since Paul died, and my married friends in the old neighborhood remain very close to me to this day. I was lucky to have them, other friends, and a great family. Still, I needed more. I expanded my support network to include some people who were single. Some of these new friends were widows, and others were divorced.

I also needed grief support to help understand how to cope after losing my husband about thirty years sooner than I had ever anticipated. I began by getting some one-on-one help from Hospice of Santa Cruz County. This type of service might also be available from your local hospice, even if the person close to you wasn't under the care of hospice before dying.

Even if support isn't offered in person, try to take a virtual session. Medical visits and therapy sessions are increasingly moving online. This can actually be convenient because you don't have to travel anywhere. Another advantage of a virtual session is that it opens up more opportunities for you to be connected with an expert of your choice who lives outside your local area.

My individual sessions many years ago were with a trained grief support volunteer for about an hour, once a week. In these sessions, I discussed what had happened during the week, my concerns, and any upcoming issues. The volunteer listened and helped to normalize what I was going through and provided guidance to make my life easier. Being listened to while I vented felt great.

I was fortunate because all these resources were available to me. Many people don't have that level of support, and it has been much more difficult for people who had to deal with loss during COVID-19 shutdowns. Fortunately, there are still many resources that might be available in your community or nearby.

Places of worship have opened up again in most communities throughout the United States, at least for outdoor services, and people are once again connecting with their religious community. Social services in some areas are starting to offer in-person help—something that was put on hold for so long. Many community centers are opening their doors again, often with limited capacity and other restrictions, and many people are slowly getting back to some of the routines they had pre-pandemic in certain locations.

While I'm a strong advocate of grief support groups, you may not be ready to enter a group session right away. You might discover that one-on-one support is more valuable in the beginning. This is particularly common in cases where the loss is so great and traumatic, and you're not ready to share it and listen to other people's problems.

When I lost Paul and finished attending the individual sessions, I participated in a grief group focused on the loss of a spouse or partner. Check with your local hospice to see if it has special groups for people based on their specific loss, such as partner, parent, sibling, and child. The support group provided an excellent opportunity to learn how to deal with my grief.

I also met a great friend in the grief group, Angie, who lost her husband around the same time I did. Her loss was tragic—a sudden heart attack. Our children were about the same age. We had a lot in common, and we made it a point to meet once a week for dinner, which we did for many years. Angie and I called this "friend therapy." It has been fifteen years since we met, and we still get together when we can.

Ultimately, I felt compelled to give back to the organization that had done so much to help me and my family. I thought that if I could be trained to lead grief groups and work one-on-one to help others heal, then something positive could result from Paul's death.

I was accepted into the volunteer grief support program of Hospice of Santa Cruz County, and my involvement with hospice had a profound positive impact on my life in many ways. In 2008, almost two years after Paul's passing, I went through grief support training. I continue to participate in the ongoing professional development sessions that hospice offers and to lead grief groups.

Your grief support volunteer or counselor may recommend other resources to help you. Some situations, based on the type of loss and your own circumstances, may be helped by seeing a licensed therapist or psychiatrist. Remember, you don't have to deal with your grief alone, even if you don't have a family, your good friends live far away, or you feel totally isolated. There are many community services available, regardless of your income. Call or visit your local city community center online to learn more about their services.

Grieving Despite an Unhappy Relationship

Many people in grief groups or who get counseling are there because they're devastated that they've lost someone and can't imagine being without them. Some people, however, are grieving, and they don't know why. They may have been in unhappy or even unhealthy relationships that they stayed in because it was just too much effort emotionally and financially to leave. They may have completely grown apart, but remained a couple for the sake of their children. Or they may have lost a parent or sibling whom they never really got along with and can't comprehend their own feeling of loss.

When they attend grief groups, it may be difficult because they're sad and often "stuck," but they don't miss the person who died. And they tend to feel guilty about having those emotions when others express true love for the person they lost. Here's the truth: even if your relationship was rocky, there are a number of reasons why you're grieving. Grief support can help you too.

Here are some points to consider.

1. You mourn what could have been. There was likely a time when you had a dream for your relationship and that it would work out successfully. When that person is gone, you realize that it's too late to change things.

2. You mourn the old times when the relationship was good. You feel guilty that you weren't able to make it any better over time. Now it's too late.

3. You miss what's familiar. Your relationship was far from perfect, yet you may cling to what is known. Now that the structure of your life has changed, you'll likely deal with a lot of unknowns. You'll need to take risks to move forward, and you may not feel ready to do that.

4. Other family members and friends may be grieving, and you might have to deal with their loss too. Perhaps you and your mom didn't get along with each other, but your children loved her and miss her. You may struggle with conflicted feelings of relief mixed with guilt and worry about how those feelings affect your relationships with other family members.

5. Your lifestyle may change if you were financially dependent on that person. If you stayed in an unhappy relationship but managed to maintain a lifestyle that was comfortable, you may find yourself

having to relocate, scale back, or make other sacrifices to deal with financial pressures that arise.

If you were a stepparent and your spouse, the breadwinner, left everything to his kids, in some states you might find yourself having to move out of the house where you're currently living and start over.

Or, you miss your father, but your relationship was fraught with challenges, and you resent how he handled his finances. Perhaps you are angry that your father left his money to your stepmother instead of you. That could make you feel unloved by your dad. You may not realize that at seventy-five, the stepmother may have few, if any, employment options and needs a financial cushion in case she becomes ill.

6. Your role has changed, and the responsibility is overwhelming. You and your spouse or partner may have drifted apart over the years, yet you stayed together because it was too much effort to maintain the household if you lived apart. Now you'll have to be responsible for the things that person managed — taking care of the kids, planning activities, assuming full responsibility for family meal preparation, paying the bills, and so on.

7. You feel guilty about being relieved. Perhaps that person had a substance abuse or alcohol problem that put a tremendous strain on the relationship. You wanted out of the relationship but didn't end it. When that person died, you were freed of the burden of never knowing what type of mood you would need to cope with when you arrived home from work. Would it be a good day or a bad one? You may be angry at yourself for feeling relieved.

8. You mourn the years lost trying to make it work.

Here's an example of how a sister managed to deal with loss after her estranged sister died by suicide.

Cindy never got along with her sister, Stephanie, and as the only remaining living relative, was tasked to put Stephanie's affairs in order after Stephanie died by suicide during the peak of the pandemic. It was an unpleasant and emotionally charged ordeal.

Cindy was always the responsible one in the family and her sister had spent a good part of her adult life in and out of rehab programs for drug addiction. Cindy's husband felt sorry for Stephanie, but he was actually relieved when she died. He said it was because he and Cindy would no longer have to deal with threatening calls in the middle of the night, chaos, and all the other drama that happens when someone is addicted to drugs.

Cindy blamed herself for not being able to get Stephanie to change when she was alive. She invited Stephanie on trips, only to be disappointed by Stephanie's disruptive behavior. Yet Cindy wondered, "Why am I so sad? I couldn't help Stephanie and she's no longer in pain."

Through therapy Cindy realized that she was mourning what could have been. She was grieving the loss of the sister she wanted Stephanie to be. As Cindy took out pictures of Stephanie from their youth, she remembered the good times they once shared and was comforted. She put those pictures on the wall and tried to focus on those positive moments and memo-

ries. Cindy couldn't change the outcome and what happened to Stephanie, but at least she changed her outlook and focused on remembering better times.

If you find yourself grieving the loss of someone, even though the relationship was often unpleasant, consider getting one-on-one assistance from a professional to make you feel more comfortable about moving forward and letting go of self-critical or conflicted feelings.

Visiting Familiar Places

When you were a couple or part of a family, chances are that you had a favorite restaurant, wonderful memories of places that you visited, and local shops that you went to regularly. Going to these locations alone now might be comforting, but in many cases, it can cause emotional stress that you hadn't anticipated.

Be prepared for an unexpected reaction when you initially return to these places on your own. It may take time before you feel at ease in these settings.

Before Paul was diagnosed with cancer, I remember our routine of going to the grocery store together after breakfast on Saturday mornings. At the time we had this weekly errand, I never thought of the experience of trudging through a grocery store as one that was particularly bonding or fun. It was just another chore to do on my day off from work. I went because he wanted me to join him, even though it always took twice as long when we did this together as when I shopped alone.

It wasn't until he died that I realized how much I missed our trips to the store. About two weeks after his death, I walked into the store with tears in my eyes, knowing that this simple routine would never be the same. I thought of all the times I grudgingly joined Paul, and I wished I had appreciated our time together. It was so lonely walking into that familiar place without him.

As I moved my cart down one of the aisles, I heard a couple fighting. I walked over to them and said, "Are you married?" When the wife answered yes, I looked this stranger in the eyes and said, "Both of you should stop fighting and hug instead. Be grateful that you have each other. I used to come shopping here every week with my husband, but I can't do that anymore because he just died." The couple looked at me, speechless. Then they hugged each other and thanked me for reminding them of the importance of being together.

Maybe after I left, they spoke about the crazy woman who had barged in on their argument and told them what to do. Either way, it made me realize how much I missed the ordinary activities with Paul and that I needed to adjust to that change.

I decided to wait a few months before returning to that store again. It wasn't because I was embarrassed that I yelled at strangers. It was because I knew that I had to wait until I was comfortable walking in there alone. When I was finally emotionally able to return to the store, I made it a special point to avoid going there on Saturday mornings.

Several months after Paul died, my daughter went off to college. It was the first time I wanted to enjoy having a special dinner at my favorite restaurant and was able to go there by myself. While this sounds like something that should be easy to do, it wasn't. Like many widows of my generation (Baby Boomers), I had always lived with someone—parents, roommates, a husband, and children.

I brought a newspaper with me to the restaurant, ordered dinner, and even though I felt lonely being there without Paul, I got through the meal alone. I promised myself that if I ever visited any of our old favorite places and felt uneasy, I would just bring a friend. Or I'd avoid those venues until I was ready. By the time I was prepared to go to places like that alone, I actually enjoyed the experience. I got to eat what I wanted, when I wanted, and sit quietly, reading a newspaper, which I found was very relaxing.

Now, think about what happens when you return to your favorite vacation locations without that person who was close to you. My sons took me on a family vacation to a place I used to visit with Paul. I was so grateful to be with them, one of my daughters, and my daughter-in-law. It was a break from my routine and an opportunity to reflect on what mattered, but it's not always practical—from a time, logistics, or financial standpoint—to use that experience as a tool for healing.

Of course, travel can be complicated as we work through the pandemic, and the guidance for travel is currently fluctuating due to how COVID-19 is affecting certain areas. You can also achieve similar, positive results by connecting with people in an environment that gives you a break from your everyday life.

When you are able and feel comfortable enough to travel, consider visiting someone you know in another city. Or tour with a group (assuming group tours are available to your desired destination), and use that time to also reflect on what's meaningful to you. Think about visiting a local park, museum, or anywhere you can relax. If you live near a beach, lake, river, pond, or other area surrounded by natural beauty, take advantage of it.

If you're someone who must constantly check your phone, try turning it off during these decompression adventures. It's difficult to relax if you feel bombarded by texts, emails, or alerts. While cell phones and text messages are great for staying connected, they also may exacerbate anxiety when you need time to breathe and be fully present to enjoy your surroundings. Sometimes it's helpful to disconnect from technology for brief periods, even if it's just a few hours, especially when you're traveling and want some quiet time. If you haven't finished this book, consider bringing it along on a trip and reading it. Or take another book that appeals to you.

At some point, you may even visit a familiar vacation spot or local attraction with a friend, relative, or potential future relationship. Be aware that you need to be prepared for those outings, depending on the memories that they elicit.

My stepfather died suddenly in 2018, and I recall going to Jack London Square in Oakland with him on several occasions. I still get a little emotional when I walk by his favorite restaurant there. Those emotions are more bittersweet. I don't cry. Instead, I think about how nice it would be if he could join us and focus on fond memories of his visits.

Sometimes you may feel okay returning to a familiar place.

Barry's wife, Charlotte, died during the pandemic, and he stayed home for months during the lockdowns. A friend called Barry six months later, and the topic came up about how much Barry liked to take group dance lessons with Charlotte. His friend said, "Why don't you go back to the dance studio and give it a try?" Barry was nervous but desperately needed to get out of the house. To his surprise, he discovered that dancing gave him a glimmer of happiness. He danced with the instructor and other people in the class. Of course he missed dancing with Charlotte, but returning to a familiar place and getting a little bit outside his comfort zone was just what he needed.

Not everyone is like Barry. Sometimes you have to ease into visiting familiar places where you had happy memories with the person you're grieving. Just give yourself enough time and proceed cautiously. Understand that you may feel a mix of sadness and joy, yet know that engaging in these adventures should get easier and will be more enjoyable as time goes on.

Memorial Services, Funerals, and the Need for Closure

In many religions, the service must happen soon after the death. Some religions offer more flexibility on when a service should occur. Planning a service may seem overwhelming when you just lost someone close to you, and it may be more convenient to wait a month or more.

A significant delay, however, can cause people to get "stuck" and extend the denial phase of grief. That's what happened to so many people who never got a chance to have a traditional service during the pandemic. They didn't get that opportunity to be comforted, hugged, and give or attend a ceremony in honor of the deceased individual. Some people even lost multiple members of their families to COVID-19 and never got to work through their grief after the first person who died before losing another.

I remember watching a video memorial service of Paul's mom, who died during the early COVID-19 lockdowns in her community in 2020. If this had happened at another time, I would have been on a plane immediately to see her and attended the service to pay my respects to this wonderful woman. The service was small, and I watched it from my computer. I missed out on the chance to comfort other family members in person. When a sister-in-law of mine died in late December 2020, her husband also had a small service. Again, I felt like they were cheated and so were we, because we couldn't physically be there to honor her. At least they both had a service, even if it wasn't the big family gathering that would've taken place if we weren't in the middle of a pandemic.

Based on my observations, however, I can understand how it helps to have any type of service, even if it's just a small group of people on Zoom, within a reasonable time after someone dies. Some people I know who didn't have a service for their loved one became deeply depressed after that loss.

Even months after someone close to them died, well before the pandemic, they still hadn't gotten around to it for various reasons. It was too difficult to get the family together and coordinate everyone's schedules. Their work was too demanding. They wanted to wait for summer, when the weather was nicer, and so on. When they finally had a service, however, it seemed to help comfort them. Plus, they generally became less anxious and more engaged with other people, the tasks ahead of them, and new activities.

If you would have been responsible for setting up a service for someone who died during or before the pandemic — and it was too difficult to get it done at the time — think about having some type of gathering now. Keep in mind that it doesn't have to be a major event. It could be as basic as getting a small group of family and friends together for a simple ceremony outside. You may be surprised by how much the act of being surrounded by people to support you helps to give the strength necessary to move forward.

When Karen's father died, her husband led a service in the senior home where her dad had lived. People gathered, shared stories about him, and celebrated with cake, coffee, and cookies. It was a modest and dignified tribute that was done in a timely manner, and it helped bring her family together. Another woman I know took her children on a boat ride to her late husband's favorite place, a local lake, where they said prayers and honored him.

Some religions have additional services a year after a person's death. Experiencing another service a year later may be part of your tradition. You may find this comforting, or one service may be all that you can handle. You'll determine which approach is best for you, based on your unique needs and your religious beliefs.

These are just recommendations, and I recognize that there are people who prefer not to have an official service. If that's not what you need, don't feel pressured into having one.

Working through grief is a complicated process. By journaling, releasing anger, getting help, forgiving yourself and others, and following some of the other suggestions I've discussed, you can help to ease the pain of grief.

4

Gaining Insight and Planning for Better Days Ahead

When Paul was ill, a hospice social worker said to me, "Hospice can be beautiful." I thought, *Are you crazy? My husband is dying. What can be beautiful about that?*

Many months after Paul passed away, I finally figured out what the social worker was trying to convey. Hospice care gave Paul the opportunity to be in his own home and get guidance from the hospice chaplain. It enabled me to play a role in keeping him calm during this difficult time. I discovered depths of love that I never thought were imaginable. I read stories to him each night, some that I had written. We savored every moment when he was well enough to walk, talk, eat, and visit with friends and family. We cherished his good days and appreciated simple things, like being able to take a ride in the car to look at the outside scenery or to listen to music at home.

Paul told me about his dreams of pages on calendars breaking away, an indication that he was running out of time. By watching him die, I realized how important it was to focus on finding simple joys in life after his passing. I stopped complaining about petty issues related to people and politics.

It was no longer worth it to sweat the small stuff or become annoyed when I got stuck in traffic. I became a calmer and more patient person most of the time. I remembered to slow myself down, and I made it a point to thank people for their kindness, whether it was my friends, co-workers, or the clerk at the grocery store who packaged my purchases.

After coping with the COVID-19 shutdowns, quarantine requirements, and forced isolation for so many people, you've probably arrived at a similar conclusion. No matter how difficult it has been moving through various ups and downs during the pandemic, you have found ways to get through it. And for so many people, this time is much more challenging than what I had experienced during Paul's loss. Many of you may have had to do caregiving from a distance—providing connection and reassurance only by phone or online, even when you might have lived nearby the person who was sick.

Even if you had the resources to hire a caregiver to assist your relative, partner, or friend, it might not have been possible to find someone to help. Due to COVID-19 restrictions, you may have had to rely on the staff in a nursing home or hospital being at the bedside of your relative, partner, or friend. Instead of you, these people held that person's hand when they left this world. It's painful and makes it more difficult to work on what's next for you.

Sometimes, it's likely that you'll become more reflective about your values. Consider taking time to think about what's most important to you. Eventually, you'll find ways to make changes that will help you to lead a more fulfilling life.

Family and Friends Can Help You Cope

I'm not saying that you can change who you are overnight just because you've suffered a loss, especially as we move through the pandemic, but it's safe to assume that you'll look at the concept of time very differently when you come face-to-face with the reality that it's limited.

Where can this new insight lead you? Some people begin to reassess their priorities. For example, if spending more time with your children, grandchildren, parents, other relatives, or friends is important, then develop a plan to make that happen.

I wanted to spend more time with my adult children, growing number of grandchildren, and other family members. Many of my relatives are a long drive or plane flight away, but I try to visit with them as often as I can, whether it's virtually or in person. It's well worth the effort to stay connected.

Your calendar — whether it's on your phone, on the wall, or in a planner — can become a trusted assistant. Schedule time to be with people you enjoy. If you were a caregiver, chances are that you put many of your own priorities on hold. Now it's time to take care of yourself.

Contact the people you want to be with and arrange to see them if you feel comfortable doing so during this pandemic. For example, if you have adult children who live nearby, see if you can schedule a weekly or every other week dinner or lunch. If you have grandchildren, for example, volunteer to babysit when you can and give their parents a night out. It's amazing how healing it can be to get to know your grandkids better, and they can benefit from the attention too. The same goes for nieces, nephews, and other kids. I cherish the moments with my grandchildren, and watching them grow up brings me so much joy. If the time isn't right for in-person visits, then consider online virtual gatherings.

If you lost a parent, and especially if this was your only remaining parent, think about those people who knew your mom or dad who might provide some comfort to you. Maybe it's an aunt or uncle or long-term family friend. If your parents were divorced, and your father who recently died had a partner or wife, consider how that person might be someone who can help comfort you. If you had a good relationship with your stepparent, then you might be able to work together through this loss.

Darsha's husband, Ashish, had a stroke during the pandemic and was severely physically and mentally handicapped. Darsha was his caregiver and had always been close to Ashish's twenty-year-old daughter from a previous marriage, Kaeya, who was an only child. After Ashish passed away from complications of COVID-19, Kaeya was devastated. As difficult as it was to witness her father's decline, the reality sunk in that he was gone.

Ashish had always helped Kaeya deal with the typical decisions that young people face in their lives related to relationships, careers, finances, and so on. Who could help fill that gap? Her own mother died years before, and Kaeya didn't have any aunts or uncles to turn to. Who could help Kaeya cope with this tremendous loss? Darsha sensed this pain and reached out to Kaeya. They would get together periodically, share stories about Ashish, and become a great source of comfort to each other.

Not every family has this friendly dynamic between stepparents and children, but when this cohesiveness exists, it can be powerful, beautiful, and incredibly healing. I'm grateful that my stepdaughter and I have become so much closer over time, and this has helped both of us deal with life's challenges after loss. I think of her and refer to her as a daughter.

Make it a point to spend time with your friends. Schedule activities with them. Contact the people who are important to you and see when they might be available to meet. It will give you something to look forward to each week.

If you've lost a spouse or partner, you may have friends who also find themselves alone after being in a coupled relationship. They might appreciate the opportunity to have a companion to join them for a meal, attend an outdoor event, or even take a trip.

Before the pandemic, one woman I know got together with another widow in her neighborhood once a week. They go to each other's homes and watch movies and then discuss the plots over coffee. Your activities don't have to cost anything. You just need to find a way to connect with others. It's worth the effort. Depending on how things are opening up in your community, it should become easier to socialize with others.

Research has shown that people who are lonely are much more likely to have shorter lives than those who are actively engaged with others. Some leading studies have concluded that loneliness is a greater health risk than obesity and that social isolation can increase your mortality risk dramatically. So it's crucial for your well-being to find ways to connect, even if it's just virtually.

If you're grieving the loss of a close friend, try to engage with other friends regularly and keep an open mind about meeting new ones. I used to get together for dinner or walks once a week with my friend Kelly, and when she died suddenly of cancer, it left a big hole. Eventually, I found a few new friends. While I will always miss Kelly, and fondly remember her, I cherish my new friendships and how they play an important role in my life.

Before Kelly died, I told her that she had my blessing to spend time with Paul when she got to heaven. We joked about that and wondered what it would be like after life. What's ironic is that I got a plaque in honor of Paul in front of a redwood tree at the Hospice Grove. After Kelly died, her family purchased a plaque for her in front of the tree that's right next to his. So here on Earth they are together, and that makes me feel better.

If you're in a situation where you don't see friends and family very often, then consider joining a group of people who share your common interests. Visit Meetup.org and sign up for an activity that appeals to you. Or go to your local community center to find out about activities in your area, such as day trips, workshops, classes, exercise programs, and volunteer work. If you're not in a position to leave your home, consider taking virtual excursions or online classes.

Reinventing Yourself

Loss gives you the opportunity to reflect on who you are and what you want to do with the rest of your life, or at least for the next few months or years.

Li-Na had been her husband's caregiver for many years. During that time, she stopped working as a teacher, cut back on social engagements, and put all her energies into keeping her husband safe and comfortable. After he died, Li-Na, who was about seventy, realized that she always wanted to be an artist. She had never pursued that interest because she had been too busy earning a living as a teacher.

So Li-Na enrolled in community college art classes and hired an art tutor. Her watercolor paintings blossomed into masterpieces that were on display in local galleries, museums, and stores. She discovered that creative expression was her ticket to happiness. Today, she's very involved in the arts and participates in gatherings with other artists. Whenever I see her, she's always smiling. The artist within her emerged, and she found a talent that she never knew existed. Creating art became her new love and passion.

Healing by Making a Difference

One way to soothe grief is to get outside yourself and assist other people. That's where volunteering for an organization that you believe in can help you as much as it helps others. There are so many opportunities where you can make a difference when you're ready.

Leslie ran a printing business with her partner, Wendy, and closed the business after Wendy died. Leslie wanted to find something additional to occupy her time, help people in her community, and give her a reason to leave the house each day. About six months after Wendy's sudden death, Leslie volunteered at a local organization that provided clothing, household items, furniture, and other resources to those in need. Leslie said that the volunteer work gave her life structure, which she was missing, as well as a chance to make a difference. She also enjoyed the social contact with other volunteers and made some new friends through this organization.

Hector worked in the fast-paced, high-tech world as a chief technology officer, but he reevaluated his life after his wife died of cancer. The sixty-hour workweeks were taking a toll on his health and his ability to enjoy the limited spare time he had available. He switched careers, took a pay cut, and got a job with a forty-hour workweek for a nonprofit that provided medical services to people in need. Reducing his workload left him with more time to exercise to improve his health. Hector was proud of his new career, and he developed friendships with people at work who shared his common interests and goals.

Jasmine moved out of her apartment and put her work on hold as a restaurant manager to move in with and help take care of her best friend, Kayla, who died six months later from cancer. Jasmine and Kayla were in their early thirties, had been best friends since they were children, and were inseparable.

Kayla didn't have family to take care of her and needed full-time help and company. Kayla's community was under a complete lockdown during her illness, and Jasmine took care of her every need — arranging medical appointments, doing household chores, paying bills, and just being there as a good friend to make the best out of a sad situation.

Jasmine had been running on adrenaline just to get through each day and help her friend. When Kayla passed away, Jasmine had to take care of all the "business paperwork" related to Kayla's death, clean out Kayla's rented cottage, and find a new place to live.

Jasmine couldn't return to her old job because the restaurant where she had worked went out of business during the pandemic. Besides, she never really liked the job. It was just a means to make a living. Jasmine was surprised to learn that she inherited some money from Kayla, and it would be enough to supplement her income for a year, even if she didn't work full time.

Jasmine played the piano and had been a music teacher part-time for many years before she decided to work in the restaurant. She loved giving piano lessons and took the restaurant job because it was more lucrative. After losing her friend, she decided not to go back to the restaurant industry. She wanted to pursue something more rewarding. With the inheritance from Kayla, Jasmine was in a position to rebuild her music teaching business and pursue a career that was more meaningful — one that, in time, could also prove to be a good financial choice.

The insight you glean from your loss can shape your volunteer work, career, relationships, health, and goals. You can't make the loss go away, but you can use it to help you transform and grow.

5

GETTING BACK IN CONTROL

Your own sense of identity and the role you play in your family can change based on the type of loss you experience. Let's look at some of them.

Losing a spouse or partner is different from other losses. That person has generally been with you daily. After loss, your identity as part of a couple suddenly fades. Now it's just you. This obvious revelation didn't fully sink in for me until I filled out an application for an account and had to check "single" in the box instead of married. I thought, *How did this happen? I didn't ask to become single. I'm not ready to move into this category. Now what am I going to do?*

As difficult as it was to admit that I couldn't return to my old life, I truly empathized with many of the people a generation older than me who experienced a similar loss.

Grace lived in a home in the woods in California. She was married for sixty-five years to her high school sweetheart, and her daughter lived in Europe. She didn't have any siblings or cousins. Her husband paid all the bills, and Grace tended to the garden and household. Because her home was in a remote location, she didn't have neighbors who could look in on her. Most of her longtime friends who were still alive had moved out of state. It was a twenty-minute drive into her local town. Her eyes weren't as sharp as in the past, and she stopped driving at age eighty-five.

Grace finally realized that she needed some assistance after her husband died, but wasn't sure how to make that happen. While it's generally a good idea not to make major changes, like moving and quitting your job, until at least a year after a loss, Grace's circumstances were an exception. She couldn't afford to maintain the home on her own, and she was living in a place where her closest neighbors were about a quarter mile away. A friend suggested that Grace look into selling her home and moving to a community where she'd have a support system and would be more centrally located.

Relocating was the first major decision that Grace made on her own without her husband. She knew that it wasn't going to be easy to leave her house of many years, the home she loved. Leaving this home felt like another loss, but she believed it was the right decision. Besides, she was so lonely living in a remote environment without her husband.

With advice from experts, Grace decided to sell the house and move into a retirement community. It was difficult to leave her home and its memories and to part with many of the furnishings and items that simply would not fit in her tiny residential unit. At first, she put them in storage because she couldn't bear to give them up. After a year of paying for a storage facility, she finally realized that this was a costly decision and asked a friend to give away most of the belongings from the storage unit.

Gradually, Grace became used to the new environment and enjoyed socializing with many of the residents. She found it empowering to make her own decisions about where to live, what movie to see, and what restaurant to visit and to be unencumbered with the responsibility of maintaining a house. She learned how to pay the bills and take over responsibilities that her husband had always handled.

Ultimately, she transformed from a quiet, introverted wife, living in the country, to an outgoing woman who enjoyed socializing, visiting local museums and shops, and becoming involved in her community activities. Being on her own taught her that even though she missed her husband, she was capable of being self-sufficient and happy.

Here's another example of someone who was able to make a positive change in his life after the loss of his wife.

Henry, who owned a computer-repair shop with his wife Vicky, always wanted to return to college and get a computer science degree, but he kept putting it off due to his ongoing personal responsibilities. He worked long days to pay for their house. As his family grew, it became less likely that he'd ever have the time to attend college. There was always something that took priority over his getting a degree.

About a year after his wife died, Henry, who was forty-six at the time, decided to pursue his dream of a college degree. His kids had moved out of the house and had gone off to college. He was lonely, but for the first time in many years, he finally had enough flexibility to return to school.

Henry cut his work back to thirty hours a week and hired someone to help manage his repair business so that he could attend classes. While losing Vicky was devastating, Henry knew that he couldn't do anything to change the situation. Since his personal obligations were no longer holding him back, and he could afford to hire an assistant, he pursued his long-term goal of being a software developer. A few years after Henry returned to college, he got a degree in computer science.

Henry eventually sold his repair business. Today, he enjoys the team environment of working at a high-tech startup and the challenge of developing software. The new company he works for has a baseball team that plays on weekends, and he was excited to join the team. He likes the camaraderie of this working environment and the opportunity to develop friendships for his new life.

Anita is another example of how to find an opportunity after a loss.

Anita moved to Los Angeles to be with her partner, Dan, but never really liked the city. When her kids were growing up, Anita worked full time as a realtor and regretted not being able to attend their soccer games or school programs.

After Dan died, following a long illness, Anita eventually moved to Phoenix, Arizona, to be near her children, grandchildren, elderly parents, and siblings. It made sense financially because the cost of living was considerably less in Phoenix than in Los Angeles. Anita knew that she'd miss her friends from Los Angeles and that starting over in a new community in her sixties and building a new network of friends wouldn't be easy. To avoid rushing into making a big change, she waited more than a year after Dan died before she moved.

Relocating to Phoenix was just what she needed to rebuild her life. Anita enjoyed babysitting her grandchildren two days a week and working part-time in a bookstore. The job paid considerably less than what she had earned as a realtor in Los Angeles, but that no longer mattered to her.

The part-time job provided some income to supplement her retirement, and it freed up her time to cultivate a social network as she established herself in this new community. Babysitting the grandkids gave Anita the opportunity to experience some of what she had missed when her own children were growing up. Having her family nearby provided comfort as she dealt with the loss of her partner and began assimilating into a new environment.

When you lose a parent, your role also shifts dramatically. You may suddenly need to take on responsibilities you never imagined, whether it's looking after younger siblings, taking on more work to support your remaining parent, or having the newly widowed parent move in with you. Suddenly, you find yourself in a role that you weren't prepared for.

When Constantine's father died, he put some of his own activities on hold so that he could help out his mother, Alexandra, who had limited mobility and vision. He soon discovered that his mom was so grief-stricken that she was making impulsive decisions and spending money that she wasn't in a position to plunk down. Constantine felt that if Alexandra went way over her budget, he'd be the one who would feel obligated to take care of her, and he was already overloaded between his job and other responsibilities.

He would get calls from Alexandra at all hours of the night whenever she had a problem, whether it was a technical issue with a computer, a dispute about a bill, questions about a medical report, something broken in her house, or just a request for him to run some errands for her. Constantine was fine with helping out with errands and stopping by to check in periodically, but he also had a wife and kids and his own responsibilities. He felt guilty about feeling depressed over the loss of his dad and for resenting the added responsibilities he felt obligated to fulfill. He wanted to help his mom, but he also had to think about boundaries.

Constantine's wife struggled too. She was trying to be patient with him, but his new responsibilities put an added burden on her as well. They decided to go to couples counseling and get help with Constantine's grief and how to help his mom without jeopardizing his health, happiness, and family life.

The counselor encouraged Constantine to attend a virtual "loss of parent" grief group at his local hospice so that he could share his thoughts with people in similar situations.

She also suggested that he set boundaries with his mom and look into resources that could help her – a financial planner to provide advice related to spending, a handyman service, and a computer service expert.

She mentioned that Constantine could show his mom how to order food online from her local grocery store and have it delivered. If these services become too complicated and Alexandra appears to be lonely and not fully capable of independent living, the counselor also suggested that his mom look into relocating to a nearby senior facility at some point where everything would be readily available, and she'd be surrounded by other people to keep her connected.

By following this advice, Constantine was able to focus on coping with the loss of his father, ensure that his mom was taken care of, and deal with ways to work through his grief.

When Your Sibling Dies

If you lost a sibling, whether this happened before or during the pandemic, you may be faced with other issues. Perhaps you and your brother didn't get to spend much time together after you went off to college because he moved two thousand miles away. You may miss him and wish you had gotten to know him better as adults. So you mourn for what could have been.

Your parents are grieving, and you could find yourself working extra hard to try and make up for the fact that now you're the only adult child left. Your role has changed, and now you might feel like you have to represent yourself as well as your brother to your parents and accept all the extra responsibilities that go with this change.

How can you deal with this situation? Again, this is about doing your best but setting boundaries with your parents to protect your own well-being. Find people who have been in a similar situation and see how they coped.

"Loss of sibling" grief groups can be helpful, especially as you try to work through any potential feelings of guilt about all the things you might have done differently in the past if you had known that your brother or sister had a shortened lifespan. In these groups, you might also figure out how to address added responsibilities that your parents might have wanted you to take on, even if you weren't ready or interested in doing so.

Be Flexible and Patient with Yourself

Moving forward after a loss is a big adjustment. It may take you months, or a year or more, to think about how to reshape the direction of your life. This might involve moving, changing careers, adopting new habits, finding new friends, volunteering, setting boundaries, or getting outside help. Be patient, and set manageable expectations. Move at a pace that's comfortable.

Don't try to take on more than you can handle, or you'll get so caught up in day-to-day tasks that it will be difficult to focus strategically on what you need to do to meet your long-term goals once you're able to set them.

For at least the first six months or so after a loss, you may feel unproductive in many areas. That's to be expected because you're still absorbing the loss and adjusting to its impact. Plus, we lost a lot of time in the pandemic, not to mention dealing with the added stress, isolation, and economic disruption it has caused.

Try to plan activities a week in advance. It's helpful to build more structure into your schedule, such as taking an exercise class, even if it's online, or attending a community event a few days a week. Be sure to allow yourself enough time to decompress.

Don't underestimate the extra work you have to do now that your friend or relative isn't there to help. You may have shared chores, and now you need to carry a double load with new responsibilities. This could include having to develop skills related to bill paying, accounting, cooking, tending to a garden, or fixing broken appliances. The list goes on and on. Go easy on yourself and get help from a friend or expert when needed. In my case, I tracked down a handyman to take over a lot of the household repairs that came intuitively to Paul, but that were difficult or seemed impossible for me to do.

You can do certain things to help cope with the extra burden you face when you lose someone close to you. Set boundaries with others based on how much time you can comfortably interact with people, and prioritize your personal goals and social objectives.

- If your annual visit to see Aunt Della in another city is expensive, emotionally draining, logistically difficult, and time-consuming, tell her you simply can't make it this year, but you'll keep in touch by phone, email, or Zoom.

- If you used to cook family dinners for the holidays, and it's just too much effort, consider having someone else do that instead. When all else fails, there's always takeout. You can also divide up the responsibilities and make these events potluck, even if this needs to include individually pre-packaged food, where everybody has to bring a certain item.

- If your sister wants to visit from out of town and stay with you for two weeks, and you don't feel like company, then just say no. Explain that you're not ready for guests. Or if you are ready for guests, but just for two days, then make that perfectly clear.

Give yourself permission to do what you need to do to feel better. If that means creating space for self-discovery and grieving, so be it.

Decluttering: Addressing Physical and Emotional Challenges

I've known people who have lost their spouses or children decades ago, yet their homes, furnishings, and accessories remained stuck in time. Keeping everything the same can be comforting for a while. Ultimately, however, that can make it more difficult for some people to move forward with their lives.

Lena was forty when her husband died from cancer. For the first ten years after his death, she stayed in the same house and didn't make any changes to it. Her late husband's clothes remained in the closet she had shared with him and in the dressers in her bedroom. His pictures covered the walls, and his office remained untouched. The house was frozen in time, and Lena was lonely. Yet in those ten years, Lena never dated and rarely socialized, except for attending her children's school events. She just managed to get through each day and rarely experienced joy.

By the time Lena's kids went off to college, she decided it was time to begin socializing, even though she wasn't interested in having another relationship. When she finally met a man who had all the traits that appealed to her, Lena discovered that she was ready to engage in a social life again. But before that could happen, she thought it was important to make some changes in her environment to reflect where she was at the present, instead of living in the past. Not doing this work can keep you from having room for other opportunities.

Lena was finally able to declutter her home. She still kept pictures of her husband on the walls, but they were mainly in her spare bedroom, hallway, and office, instead of everywhere throughout the house. She redecorated the master bedroom with new accessories and gave away her husband's clothes and his items that were in the room. She turned his office into a guest room, put some of his treasured items in a box, and donated many of his other belongings to charity.

Some people declutter their household immediately after the death; others do so over time. Move at the pace that's most comfortable for you. You can find special ways and places in your home to preserve certain memories of your loved one while still making enough changes to accommodate your new situation. Here are some steps that can help you get started.

1. As soon as you feel comfortable, if you shared a room with your spouse or partner, consider emptying the master bedroom closets and drawers of your loved one's stuff. You don't have to get rid of these things right away, and you might want to keep certain items for sentimental value. For many people, though, it's too painful to look at clothes in a closet, knowing that their loved ones are not coming back.

2. Store these and other personal items in a place where you won't have to see them every day. Consider moving them temporarily to a garage if you have one. When you're emotionally ready, you can determine what you want to donate, give away to friends or relatives, keep, or sell. Also, you can always take pictures of certain sentimental items and put them in a scrapbook. The same concepts apply if you lost a parent or other people in your home. Sort through the items that you want, and then move, donate, or get rid of everything else.

3. If you lost a child or grandchild, it may be quite some time before you even feel comfortable going into the child's room. When you are ready to decide what to keep or give away, have someone there with you so that you don't have to do this alone. Some people may decide to close the door and leave the room as-is for years. If possible, consider getting some counseling to help you through this difficult process.

4. Think about changes in your environment that might give you a fresh start. Paul, for example, died in a hospital bed in our bedroom. I had trouble sleeping at night until I was able to change the look of the room. I didn't want to go to the expense of buying new furniture at the time, but I got new sheets, blankets, accessories, and a bedspread. I even painted the walls a different color.

   My friends took Paul's clothes out of the closet we shared shortly after he died, and they put them in the garage for me to deal with when I was ready. Not everyone feels comfortable making that change so soon, but it worked for me. I also bought new towels and accessories for the master bathroom.

   I still kept some pictures of Paul on walls in the house, but eventually I moved them out of the bedroom. Some people might find it more comfortable to be surrounded by those pictures everywhere. I didn't.

5. Get a big storage box or chest and keep it as a memory box. I got a five-by-three-foot chest and filled it with cards and letters that Paul had given me, pictures, various memorabilia, videos, his journals, and other items I wanted to save. I kept this big memory box in a closet and knew that whenever I needed to connect with Paul, I had one place in my home where I could go to think about him. This was really helpful, and visiting the memory box became a routine for me on his birthday, our wedding anniversary, the date of his passing, and other times.

Having a special place (the memory box) made it easier to transition to my new life because I could "visit with him" when I needed that connection or felt I wanted to share something with him. I was also able to focus more on living in the present because this box was in one central location. Although I chose to make a memory box, you might prefer creating an altar in your home or garden or some other option.

It has been more than fifteen years since he died. Over time, I've given away some mementos from that box to other family members, but I can't seem to get rid of the box. There may be a time that I want to share the remaining items with his grandchildren when they get older.

Where Do You Want to Live?

Moving to a new place provides an incentive for decluttering your life. As I mentioned earlier, it's generally not advisable to make life-changing decisions, like moving, until at least one year after your loss. That's because most people are so overwhelmed with the impact of losing someone that another big change, even if it's positive, just adds additional stress to their lives. Unless you have really good reasons to move sooner rather than later, consider waiting.

If you have children still at home, any move can be disruptive because the kids already have to get used to living without Mom or Dad. Moving creates another adjustment that they may not be prepared to deal with at the time. You and your friends may have a social network in your community, and that network can be an ongoing source of support, structure, and normalcy.

In my case, I had always intended to leave the suburbs and move to the beach after my daughter went off to college. Many of my friends and their families lived in my suburban neighborhood, but I was the only single person in our close-knit group. I stayed there for six years after Paul's death because it made more sense financially, and my daughter had a familiar place to return to when she came home to visit me.

Eventually I was able to downsize to a small townhome. I looked at a lot of properties before making my decision and walked around the new area frequently to get a feel for the neighborhood. I even talked to my prospective future neighbors to see who lived in that community and why they liked living there to determine how I would fit in. I wanted to create new memories in a different place. Fortunately, the new community provided the same type of friendly neighborhood as the one I had left.

Some people move too soon after a loss, and it's not always because they wanted to leave. Sometimes it's a matter of survival. Many senior citizens I've known have had to travel great distances from their homes after losing their spouses or partners. They relocated, out of necessity, to be near their adult children and grandchildren. While this provided a great opportunity for them to be close to family, people often made significant sacrifices. They gave up being close to longtime friends and having a home. Some moved from their homes into a smaller apartment or senior housing. Others had to sell precious items in order to pay for living expenses.

When they made new friends in these senior residences, they dealt with the emotional reality that the friends they had lunch with one day might be gone — passed away — the next. That happens more often when you reach your eighties, nineties, and beyond. Other seniors had to cope with the adjustment of moving in with their children after so many years of being independent.

During the pandemic, senior living changed a lot, and many of the social advantages of being in a group setting faded away during the lockdowns. Anyone who experienced living in one of these places at that time, or had a relative who did, knows the anguish and isolation that occurred when people were forced to stay in their rooms for months on end without visitors. That meant no more trips to the cafeteria to gather with others. Meals were delivered outside their doors.

It was a lonely, surreal time, and even more challenging for people who were grieving the loss of their spouse, partner, or anyone close to them. Those people in senior units often lived in fear that they would catch COVID-19 from their helpers, office staff, and others. And that fear was very real. Some people caught COVID-19 from their helpers and staff and didn't survive.

It's sad and ironic for people who moved into a senior home because they wanted companionship, only to discover that they were more isolated than if they lived at home alone and had more control over their lives. Fortunately, in many places, life is getting a little closer at this time to pre-pandemic conditions: people are socializing again, even if it's only outdoors or indoors with masks in small groups, and they are grateful for the company. Having routines, people around them, and activities in a safe environment will help them work through their grief.

Before you move from your current residence for economic, health, or family-related issues, ask yourself the following questions:

1. What is the financial impact of this decision?

2. Assuming that you are considering moving only because you can't afford to live in your current place on your own, have you thought about renting out a room in your home for extra income? Although this option isn't for everyone, you might like it because this provides income, and you could enjoy having the company of a roommate. Depending on where we are in the pandemic at the time, the person you choose as a roommate should follow the health protocols that are important to you.

3. What are the advantages of moving to be near family, compared with the disadvantages of giving up proximity to your friends and social network?

4. If you have children living at home, how will this move affect them?

5. Assuming that you're still working, what impact will this have on your career?

6. When you get older, will you have physical problems that make it difficult to live in a two-story home? Although this might not apply to you now, I know

many people who had to sell their two-story homes as they got older because of the difficulty of going up and down the stairs.

7. Do you need a security system to feel safe in your new neighborhood?

8. Are there people nearby who can help you in an emergency?

9. Are you close enough to services, shopping, transportation, medical care, and places with social activities? (If you move from a city where you led an active life to a remote location to be with your family, will you feel too isolated?)

10. Can you handle the upkeep of your current residence? For example, you may want to consider downsizing to a place with a smaller yard or a townhome or condo to limit the amount of yardwork and maintenance.

11. Are you moving toward something or running away from something? If the answer is the latter, what are you running away from?

Once you've made your decision to move, even if it's the best choice and you know that you will be very happy in your new residence, you may still miss the place you left behind. It takes time to adjust to change. The decision to move is a big one that shouldn't be done impulsively. However, if you made a strategic choice based on your situation, goals, and values, you just might discover that you're happier in your new environment. If you need additional advice about moving, consider reading *Retirement Savvy: Designing Your Next Great Adventure*, by Denise P. Kalm, which provides detailed suggestions to help people focus on where they should live after experiencing a major life change.

Reaching Out to Avoid Loneliness, Even When You're Afraid

Remember how easy it was to meet others when you were a child? You showed up at school, activities were planned, and you sat with many kids in the cafeteria. Perhaps you got involved in sports or scouts. There were always people around and group activities to keep you busy.

Your situation today could be much different. You may be retired, living in an isolated area, or have a job that saps too much of your energy and time. You might need to provide extensive care for your children or parents. Perhaps you must deal with your own health limitations that make it more difficult to branch out and establish new friendships and engage in new experiences. Fortunately, there are things you can do to stay active and socially involved to help avoid the pitfalls of loneliness — even if some of these activities happen virtually.

Identify Your Personal Goals

If your objective is to meet a few new, good friends a year, then make that one of your goals, and develop a strategy for meeting people.

Become involved in activities that interest you. If you like to read books, for example, contact your local bookstore and find out if there are openings at a book club in your community. Or go online and search for the name of your city and book clubs to see if there's one that you can join. One of my friends started a book club about five years ago. We meet once a month and during the lockdowns, we gathered on Zoom. We had some in-person meetings as our community was opening up, but Zoom meetings are also an option for us. Joining a book club was an excellent way to make new friends. Plus, I enjoy reading new books.

Join organizations. Another way to become engaged in activities and meet people with similar interests is through Meetup.org. A friend who was a widow enjoyed cycling but didn't want to ride alone. She went to the Meetup website and joined a local cycling club. It gave her the opportunity to become friends with new people and to exercise—a true win/ win. A college student I know who was devastated after the loss of his best friend joined a group of musicians that he found online. He's looking forward to playing at local events and meeting new people. There are events for just about any type of interest—art, music, hiking, dancing, writing, woodworking, fishing, social action, business, and so on. Take advantage of them.

Cultivate a hobby. Having a hobby can lead to new friend-ships, as in the following example.

Tim enjoyed acting in plays when he was in college thirty years ago. When his partner died, Tim felt alone without him and settled into a rut of eating fast food and spending too much time at night on the computer or watching TV. Tim's relatives lived out of state, so even though family outings were enjoyable, they occurred only a few times a year.

A friend encouraged him to take up a hobby. That's when Tim decided to join his local community theater group. Soon, he began appearing in local performances. Acting gave Tim a sense of fulfillment and provided more structure to his life. The more he became involved in acting, the more his every-

day routines became increasingly stable. His eating habits got better, and he met new friends.

Take a class. If you want to explore special classes, even if you have a college degree, consider enrolling in your local community college or attending individual workshops sponsored by your city. If you're a senior citizen, think about taking lifelong learning courses at your local college or within your community. They can provide an opportunity to learn about topics of interest to you, whether it's a foreign language, history, cooking, literature, science, or other topics. Some of the people who attend these classes may also become part of your social network.

Even if you have physical limitations that interfere with socializing, many of these challenges can be overcome. For example, if health issues prevent you from driving, then transportation services, like Lyft and Uber, can take you to events. As you get older, it may be more difficult to drive at night. Instead of staying at home, consider transportation options available in your community. In some communities, transportation services may be offered at no cost.

Many places have senior centers that offer exercise classes, luncheons, interesting speakers, workshops, and trips to local events. Before the pandemic, I encouraged the seniors in grief groups to visit these centers, which offer a social network that can provide opportunities to meet people. There are also many interesting activities available in various parts of the country that cover a wide range of interests.

When my stepfather died in 2018, we had his memorial service at a senior center where he had attended classes, led hikes, and developed friendships. I met many of those people at his service, and they offered much-needed support to my mother. She's an active member of her local center. Now that it has reopened, she appreciates the events and social activities.

Some of the people who participated in grief support workshops before the pandemic have also found comfort in going to their churches, temples, and other religious places of worship and spiritual organizations. They also offer social activities such as dinners, classes, and volunteer programs. Although they were closed during the lockdowns, people often attended virtual religious gatherings.

Healing through Volunteering, Working, and Loving Your Pet

As I discussed earlier, volunteer work offers an excellent opportunity to meet people and make a difference. If you enjoy working with children, consider volunteering at a local school, community center, or place of worship. There are mentoring programs, like the Boys and Girls Clubs, Big Brothers and Big Sisters programs, and career coaching. You might be interested in delivering Meals on Wheels to people who can't leave their homes. Or contact FeedingAmerica.org to find your local food bank, and donate your time.

Do you have a special skill, like playing the piano, cooking, singing, creating arts and crafts, writing, developing business plans, or another expertise? Look into opportunities that leverage your skills. Visit VolunteerMatch.org to learn more about volunteer opportunities in your community. Many communities have programs to help clean up the environment, make calls from your home to support causes that you believe in, serve as a veterans' benefits coach, play music for hospice patients, work with animals, and more.

If you're actively employed and work in a physical office with others (as opposed to being a telecommuter), you have the advantage of a built-in network that can provide continuity and stability. It may be difficult to go to work each day when you're dealing with loss, and in many places companies are either remote or are just starting to bring people back to the office, even if it's only for a few days a week. If your job is something that you enjoy, and you are in a supportive environment, then consider yourself fortunate. Working in a familiar environment can provide a sense of normalcy. Collaborating with others can be enjoyable, challenging, and help you to pay the bills.

A friend who had a severe case of COVID-19, and fortunately recovered, went back to work in a nursing home in 2020. If that had happened to me, I probably would've been too traumatized to return to that same environment before vaccines became available. But she explained to me that her job helped her to make a difference and that the people she supported needed her. It provided a familiar structure during a time of chaos. Her team was more like a family.

We're fortunate to have people like her and the dedicated doctors, nurses, and staff who didn't give up and instead helped us deal with this crisis. She was often the last person to be with the patients before they passed away. Despite the emotional challenges of taking care of people during some difficult times in the crisis, and watching some of them die, the work gave her a purpose and kept her motivated.

We Need Our Furry Friends

Pets can also play a key role in providing support. It's comforting to know that when you open the door to your home, your place will feel less lonely because your dog will greet you with unconditional love. Dogs are family members too, and when you're the only remaining human at home, your dog can encourage you to get outside, walk, and enjoy the fresh air. In fact, there's been a huge increase in pet adoptions since the pandemic began. This has helped people deal with isolation and provide companionship. A friend of mine who loves dogs but didn't want the full-time commitment of taking care of one decided to foster a dog instead.

I'm not advocating that you get a dog immediately because dogs are a big responsibility, but if you already have one, consider taking it to a dog park. That's another place where people congregate. It gives you the opportunity to be outside and get to know some of your neighbors.

Although I'm not much of a cat person, I've known some cats that give the same type of affection as friendly dogs. Cats also require much less maintenance. There are also other pet options to consider, like birds or rabbits.

Money Issues and Family Dynamics

Reaching out also entails dealing with complex and often difficult topics, such as making financial decisions and working through what can be emotionally charged family expectations. Let's explore some of these challenges.

Your financial situation may change dramatically after losing someone in your household. It's not uncommon to go through a huge portion of your savings to take care of someone who is dying. If that individual was previously the breadwinner, those earnings may have dissipated after a lingering illness because that person could no longer work.

Even if you were not the primary caregiver, you might have taken time off work or school, had unplanned travel expenses, and been asked to help out in ways you weren't comfortable doing while they were ill. When you combine that with the stress of losing someone you love, it can be overwhelming.

When Emily's dad, James, became ill just before the pandemic hit, Emily had to drive a few hundred miles several times a month to help her stepmother take care of James. It was exhausting. Emily, a single mom with a full-time job, had two small children whom she had to bring with her on those trips.

It was difficult enough spending her free weekends as a caregiver while she watched her father slowly deteriorate even further during each visit. Her own children couldn't understand what was happening to grandpa and why they had to be away from their friends and activities.

To add to the stress, James's home was too small for Emily and her kids to stay there, so Emily had to pay for hotels during these frequent visits over many months. These were all expenses that Emily hadn't planned on, which added to the emotional burden of losing her dad after he passed away.

Emily was in an impossible situation, and the stress took a huge toll on her emotional state and physical health. Emily never had the initial support to help her through the grieving process.

Just after the service took place, her community went into a COVID-19 lockdown. She had to work from home, watch her kids (daycare centers were closed), and use a good portion of her savings to pay for the added expenses she incurred when her father was ill. It took more than a year of ongoing virtual therapy sessions for Emily to work through the trauma and loss associated with her father's passing while also taking care of her kids and trying to hang on to her job.

There's no quick fix for addressing Emily's struggles, but by concentrating on her ultimate goal — to focus on her kids and her own well-being — she was able to get through this extremely challenging ordeal. Having the ongoing virtual support sessions gave her the opportunity to realize that she wasn't alone, and that she didn't have to solve everything at once.

Emily tried to do one thing each day that would bring her closer to her goal. This included joining a day-care "pod," where her kids would be watched by a local mother and spend time outdoors with a few other children their age. As her community opened up, Emily was able to visit with her friends. She looked at her monthly budget and began to rebuild her savings account by carefully watching her spending. Emily joined a virtual grief group for loss of parents and became involved in her local church. All these actions helped Emily slowly put her life back together.

What happens if you were the primary caregiver and have to deal with costly medical bills, outside care, and insurance? If the person who died had a long career ahead, there's a remaining lifetime of lost income that you had expected.

To make matters worse, if you've been out of the workforce for a long time or aren't in a position to work, your lifestyle may have to change dramatically in ways you hadn't imagined. That's why it's so important to plan how to deal with them.

Lisa's husband, Al, died by suicide, and Lisa had to cope with the emotional and financial impact of his death. Al had a debilitating but not life-threating illness and was being treated for depression. When suicide is the cause of death, the loss can be even greater because the survivor may go through the trauma of thinking that there was something they could have done to prevent this outcome.

People often blame themselves for things that were not their fault or under their control. Lisa went through extensive therapy to deal with the trauma of this tragic loss. Six months later, she also joined a grief group.

With the help of a friend who was also a financial adviser, Lisa looked at her options. Because the death was a suicide, Lisa wasn't entitled to life insurance. She had gone through most of their savings during his illness and realized that she couldn't afford the full monthly payment of her home on her current salary. She was in no position, emotionally or physically, to take on the responsibility of finding a second job or looking for another one with a higher salary. She needed an extra six hundred dollars a month to stay in her home and maintain her existing lifestyle.

The adviser gave her a suggestion: rent out the downstairs bedroom. Having a roommate wasn't anything that Lisa had originally considered, but eventually she decided to do this because she wasn't ready to sell her house, move, or look for another job. After screening numerous applicants, she selected Sally. As it turned out, she and Sally became friends. Lisa enjoyed having company, and Sally lived there for many years before Lisa got a new job, sold the house at a nice profit, and downsized.

Loss creates circumstances for which you likely are not prepared, but if you keep an open mind, you can work through them.

Dean, who relied on his Social Security checks as his main source of support, lived in a one-bedroom apartment with his partner, Jake. After Jake passed away from cancer, Dean was concerned because the mounting costs for home health-care workers, which weren't covered by Medicare, had eaten away at his savings. He had no financial flexibility to pay for anything beyond routine bills. Dean, a retired carpenter, was eighty years old. His options for making a living were extremely limited, and he was on the verge of being evicted.

Dean was fortunate that he could move in with his nephew's family. It was an adjustment to make that change. Dean was determined to do whatever he could to repay his nephew, Ernie, for his generosity. Although Dean was still grieving the loss of his partner, he discovered that being surrounded by family gave him something to look forward to each day. He walked the kids to school, did repairs on Ernie's house, and babysat for the family. It wasn't the life he'd planned, but Dean made it work.

Here's another situation where life got complicated for the surviving partner during a loss that happened before the pandemic.

When Ellen's partner, Irv, passed away from a sudden heart attack, Irv's adult children inherited the house where Ellen and Irv had lived. They told Ellen that she had four months to either leave or purchase the house from them. Irv's children needed to sell it quickly because they couldn't afford the mortgage and costs of maintaining the place. Ellen didn't have the money to buy the house from them. Irv and Ellen were together for four years, but Irv never got around to setting up a life estate for Ellen.

Ellen had left a great job in England five years earlier to move to San Francisco and join Irv. Although Ellen had some savings and a satisfactory job in San Francisco, she wasn't in a position to buy the house. She loved living in San Francisco and looked at other options, such as renting an apartment, but the cost of living there was well beyond what she could afford.

Ultimately, Ellen decided to move back to England, where she could be close to her siblings, parents, and longtime friends. Eventually, she got a new job in England, but she had to cope with losing Irv and leaving a city she loved.

This is a common and very complicated situation involving stepparents and heirs.

When Susan and Larry got married, it was the second marriage for both of them. Larry and Susan each had two adult children from prior marriages. Susan was a widow, and Larry had been divorced for more than ten years. Larry moved into Susan's home, and they combined assets and created a trust and will. When Larry passed away, the entire estate went to Susan, who updated her will based on the plans she had made with Larry. The will gave half of the estate to Larry's children and the other half to Susan's children, upon Susan's death.

Larry's adult children didn't want to wait to receive money from their estate. They had economic and career struggles and felt that the money should be given to them now when they needed it the most. Conversely, Susan's adult children felt that if Larry's "kids" were going to get an advance, then they should get an advance on the inheritance at the same time.

This whole situation was very upsetting to Susan, who was trying to cope with the stress of losing her husband. It seemed like the adult children were too focused on money. Besides, Susan was approaching eighty. She was concerned that if she gave away too many assets in advance, there wouldn't be enough for her if she ever needed 24/7 health care.

These were all legitimate concerns. Ultimately, Susan decided to keep peace in the family and to help those who truly needed it. She was willing to give each adult child on both sides of the family the same amount in advance each year, rather than giving to some now and not others. Of course, if any family member wanted to delay an advance, that was fine too. Susan was also careful to limit the amount of the distributions to ensure that she could live the rest of her life without worrying that she'd run out of money to support her lifestyle.

Susan realized that her children and stepchildren were also grieving the loss of Larry. She continued keeping up the family traditions after Larry's death, such as getting everyone together for gatherings at certain times of the year. She stayed in close contact with all of her children and Larry's. Susan tried to think about what Larry would have done to maintain harmony in the family and how he would have dealt with any pressing issues and ensured that everyone was treated fairly.

The impact of the COVID-19 pandemic has increased awareness of why you need to be more proactive about what you'd like to see happen after you die. It's a very tough, emotionally challenging subject, and people don't like to discuss it, but it's important to consider when you feel ready to address this. If you're the survivor, you may need to look at updating your will and trust or creating one. An attorney who specializes in estate planning can help you. Even if you don't have much money, there may be special items you'd like to pass on to friends, relatives, or organizations. That can be incorporated into your will.

If you and your husband, for example, were each other's executor and trustee, pay special attention to whom you name as the successor in those roles when you die and who should have the power of attorney for financial matters and health care decisions. When there are many children and stepchildren involved, the decisions you make could mean the difference between having everyone get along or creating family feuds.

It's a good idea to discuss the details of your intentions for your will and trust (if you decide to have one) with your children and stepchildren if you're in that situation. Consider their feedback and ask your attorney for recommendations. If any of your potential heirs don't get along, or if you have concerns about putting certain family members in these roles, you might consider having an independent third party handle these functions. You obviously need to look at the costs and get recommendations if the independent party isn't someone you know.

Many people are uncomfortable even thinking about, let alone discussing, the status of their estate with family members. As a lone survivor, talking about what happens after you pass away may be a difficult topic to bring up. There's sometimes a fear that family members will start to make judgments or negative comments about how you spend your money. There's also the fear of losing control over your assets or having someone else make decisions about the care you'll receive if, in the future, you're not able to make these decisions for yourself.

However, failure to be transparent, regardless of your concerns, can cause family conflicts that you may not have imagined. You may be concerned, for example, that your daughter has economic needs that your son doesn't have, and you want to leave a significantly greater portion of money to your daughter. Or maybe one child has been very supportive and helpful, and the other has had a more distant relationship with you.

If you avoid discussing these issues, your family members won't have the opportunity to ask questions about special items, accounts, or your health care desires in advance. That approach can create lingering hurt feelings and conflict between your survivors, especially at a time when they are grieving.

If you meet with your children to discuss the reasons why you've made your decisions, at least you can get their input. Your son might tell you that he understands why you left more money to his sister. In fact, he may already be helping her because he's in a position to do so. Without having this conversation, however, your son might feel slighted and hurt. He might never realize what motivated your decision, other than his erroneous perception that you loved your daughter more than you loved him.

People aren't mind readers. Don't leave them guessing about why one sibling was treated one way, and the other was treated another. Some people choose to keep their financial details a secret because of the worry that if family members know they will receive an inheritance, they might spend money foolishly now and have an entitled mindset. It's a good idea to explain that you expect them to continue to be self-supporting, manage their finances effectively, and live within their means, regardless of what they might hope to receive.

Explain your values and expectations. What should you tell them? Let's look at your financial and health issues separately. For financial issues, gather information about your assets, liabilities, will, trust (if you have one), plans, and intentions. Share what you're comfortable sharing with your family members, and give this and any other relevant information to your lawyer or trusted adviser. Let your beneficiaries know the people to contact for your accounts and policies. Remember that they will be grieving when you pass away. Do what you can now to make the process less painful for them.

Even if you don't want to go into detail about the state of your finances, at least find out if there's something that they would want so that family members don't fight over Dad's car, Mom's watch, who has to take care of your dog, and so on. They might want to know where to find a list of your friends to contact. If they inherit property, they'll need to know account information about loans, bills related to the property, life insurance policies, and so on.

It's emotionally draining and time-consuming to plan what happens after you pass away or become ill and need assistance, especially while you're grieving the loss of your loved one, but it's one of those tasks that needs to be addressed before it's too late.

What to Do about Your Own Medical Priorities

Now, let's look at how you expect your designees to deal with your health care–related issues. If the person who died was your designee on your advance-care directive for your health care, be sure to update that document with the names of the people you want to handle this for you. Discuss this responsibility with them first to make sure that they will accept it.

It's important to complete an advance-care directive, because when you need care, this document will help ensure that it's done according to your wishes. Your local hospice may have forms and educational sessions on completing this document. Estate-planning attorneys can also help. Fill out the forms, along with the phone numbers of people to contact in an emergency, and put these on your refrigerator or some place that is easily visible. Make sure that your designees also have information about your long-term health care policy if you have one.

They should know the medications you take and the dosage, as well as the contact information for your doctors. If you have a neighbor or friend who checks in on you regularly, share this information with your designees and neighbor or friend. Make sure that they exchange phone numbers in case of an emergency.

There are times when family members turn against each other because they were disappointed in the way the estate was handled or because certain relatives were put in a position of trust but betrayed the wishes of the departed. If you're concerned about what will happen when you pass away, give these decisions a lot of thought. Consult with advisers you respect, family members, and even therapists, who might be able to provide more insight into this important matter.

Understanding Emotional Triggers

The first year after a loss is particularly difficult because you're bombarded with so many changes, and you're not sure how certain milestones (your anniversary, birthdays, holidays, etc.) or other situations will affect you. Of course, during COVID-19, so many of the support systems and people who would have helped you in normal times may not have been available. Whatever was available was likely limited.

If you're prepared, however, you can turn a potentially difficult situation into a memorable and positive experience. For example, the year Paul died, I became increasingly nervous as his birthday approached. How could I possibly face his birthday without him? Then the answer dawned on me—*I'll give him a party.*

Suddenly, I changed the dynamics of that day from one of dread to an event that I looked forward to hosting. I invited the friends who had helped to cook our family meals while he was sick, did errands, visited, and provided emotional support to help me through his illness. I asked them to think about a humorous or interesting memory of Paul that they could share, and I brought a photo album with pictures of him to the dinner. We ate his favorite food and toasted him, and the day turned into a wonderful celebration and an opportunity to thank many of the people who had been so helpful when I needed their support.

I've shared this experience, and people have told me that taking this perspective on an upcoming birthday was very helpful to them. Some of them decided to have small celebrations with a few members of their family to get through similar milestones. Others visited places that their loved ones enjoyed, such as the beach and hiking trails, and brought friends and family there.

In 2021, two of my relatives, who both died in 2020 during the pandemic lockdowns, coincidentally shared the same birthday. The family was scattered throughout the country, and so I suggested that we honor them with a virtual gathering that day on Zoom. We shared some memories and got a chance to check in on one another as well. The virtual "celebration" helped bring us together and make what could have been an emotionally challenging day much better. One friend I know "adopted" an elderly woman whom she invited over for a Christmas dinner. It was comforting for both of them, and it helped my friend to feel less lonely after her mom had died.

Think about ways to honor the person you miss if that's something you feel will be comforting. Every year for the past fifteen years, I've tried to do something to preserve Paul's memory on his birthday. For example, he loved driving along Highway 9 in Santa Cruz through the redwoods. I've taken that drive, listened to the music he enjoyed, and stopped off at the redwood forest—his favorite place. More recently, I established a different tradition. I eat his favorite food—pizza and an ice cream sundae. I've shared this memorial ritual with family members and some of his friends, and this has become an annual practice for many of us each year.

The first wedding anniversary after your spouse has died is likely to be the most difficult one, so I encourage you to think about it in advance and consider spending that time with friends or family. If you prefer to be alone, be extra kind to yourself that day and know that you will get through it.

A friend lost her husband around the same time that Paul died. We decided to take our daughters out to dinner on one of those early anniversaries and tried to make the best of it. The waitress looked at us innocently and said, "Are you celebrating a birthday?" My friend looked at her and said, "Not exactly. We're celebrating a death day." The waitress stared at us and looked horrified until we explained that this dinner was how we'd decided to honor our late husbands on that day.

I was surprised to discover that happy occasions can also trigger loss because that special person isn't there to share those moments with you. When Paul's son got married to a very nice woman, many years after Paul died, I wasn't prepared for my reaction. I looked at all the people at the reception and ran out of the room to a quiet place and just started to cry. It was the same type of reaction I had when, decades before, my daughter went to her first ballet recital and my father wasn't alive to share the day.

Getting back to the wedding, it was totally out of character for me to get that emotional so long after Paul was gone. I was sad because it seemed unfair that Paul wasn't alive to share in this joyful event. After composing myself, I rejoined the group and was able to take part in the remainder of the celebration. Sometimes you just don't know when something will trigger an emotion that you aren't expecting. Understand that these emotions are a normal part of grief.

The experience at that wedding made me realize that when my daughter got married two years later, I would have to contain those emotions and focus on enjoying the moment. I distinctly remember when she was seventeen, shortly after Paul died, and she burst into tears, saying, "But who will walk me down the aisle when I get married someday?" That problem was solved. I proudly and happily took over and escorted her down the aisle. The tears I experienced were those of joy, not of sadness, because I had already worked through that emotion at her stepbrother's wedding.

Another trigger is attending a funeral or memorial service for someone other than the person you're grieving.

Gloria's husband, Michael, died just a few months before her good friend's husband, Juan, passed away. Gloria was able to hold back the tears and give a powerful message at her own husband's service. I knew, however, that she was keeping a lot of emotions inside and was still working through the initial shock of Michael's death.

I gave Gloria some advice to help her get through Juan's service, which was a ninety-minute drive from her home. I told Gloria to be prepared for reliving her own grief and dealing with emotions that she might not have been able to express during Michael's memorial service. I reminded her that attending Juan's service could be unsettling. I asked her to find out who was going from her area so that she could get a ride from them. Driving in New York is hectic enough, and combined with the prospect of an emotionally laden event, she could have put herself at risk.

Gloria cried throughout Juan's service, giving herself permission to release the emotions she had suppressed at her own husband's memorial gathering. She was relieved that she attended the service with a friend and didn't have to drive home alone.

Gloria's situation is another example of knowing that certain milestones or events, like weddings and funerals, can trigger unexpected emotions. It's important to be present at these events, but she was prepared. Understand that your reactions are normal and think about a plan for how to deal with them.

The husband of a friend died early in 2021. She decided to wait to have a small family service just as her community was beginning to open up so that she could to take a few family members on a boat for a memorial service at sea. The service was much smaller than one that would have happened in normal times, but it was just right for her and her family. By being flexible, she was able to have a meaningful service that helped her and enabled other relatives to comfort each other and pay their respects.

I recently went to an in-person memorial service for the husband of another friend who was ill before and during the COVID-19 pandemic. She waited about a month and had the service as soon as it was possible to gather outdoors safely. Some family members and friends attended. What stood out for me was the powerful healing process of this ceremony. My friend and her family gave poignant speeches about the wonderful man who passed away. I didn't know him that well, but being there, looking at his pictures and listening to stories about what a great man he was, made me realize that these services not only help the family. They also give people who attend more insight into what made the person so special. Having this ritual is more than comforting the people who are grieving. It's also a way to honor, enlighten others, and pay tribute to someone. It keeps their memory alive.

If you never got to give that special person the kind of service that you wanted because of all the challenges during COVID-19, think about what you can do to help fill that potential void. Maybe it's something as simple as a Zoom, Skype, or other virtual gathering with people you want to invite to share memories. Or, perhaps, plan to have small gatherings. Maybe you just need to write about what that person means to you and share that story with people that matter. Think of what approach would work best for you and try to make it happen.

I developed this checklist to help you cope with emotionally laden milestones and situations that could set off feelings of loss.

- **Weddings and Graduations:** Focus on the joy of the day. Write down in advance what you can do if you're overcome with regret that your loved one can't experience these events. Perhaps write a letter to your friend or relative before you go, explaining why you're sad they can't experience this event. It helps to understand those feelings so that you can work them out in advance.

- **Funerals and Memorial Services:** If you're attending a service too soon after your loss, consider whether you're emotionally ready to be there. Determine if the benefits of attending outweigh the feelings of being uncomfortable. Many people find these events healing, and in Gloria's case, it helped her to work through the unprocessed grief of her husband.

- **Births and Other Happy Events:** Journaling can help. Write a letter to your relative or friend and explain how you felt when watching the birth of your grandchild or attending the child's sporting event, confirmation, baptism, bar mitzvah, or other ceremony. If this child was a descendant of the person who passed away, describe how this child may have inherited a particular talent or trait from that person, who helps keep their memory alive through the generations.

- **Day-to-Day Difficulties:** It's common to experience times when we wish our relative or friend could be there to guide us through a career crisis, health issues, or concerns about children, grandchildren, parents, siblings, and other relationships; or to give advice on practical things, like buying a new car.

  Even if you don't journal regularly or you stopped journaling many years ago, write a letter to your deceased relative or friend and ask them what you should do. If you're not into writing, just ask yourself how this person would help you solve this problem. If you're not sure, and you still need assistance, check in with someone who knew your friend or relative well. One widower kept wondering why his stepchildren would call him frequently with questions about how to deal with basic situations he thought they should be able to resolve on their own. He was the person who had been closest to their mom. So instead of considering it annoying, he could have taken it as a compliment that they trusted him enough to ask for his advice.

- **Special Songs:** Nothing seems to bring back old memories more than familiar songs. You could be enjoying a pleasant drive in the car along a scenic route, and then suddenly, the song that represented something special about that person starts playing on the radio. You might find it comforting to hear that music, but those songs can also make you cry. Stay with your emotions and know that the music you shared can create a response that could catch you off guard. Over time, it could bring a smile to your face.

As you begin to take control and proactively address these challenges, you can become more confident in your ability to move forward and adjust to the new normal. Loss can involve dealing with many different issues related to your living situation, finances, activities, memories, and relationships. Prioritize how you will manage these changes. Don't overextend yourself. Avoid making too many decisions too soon.

6

SOCIALIZING AND TRAVELING

Depending on where you are in your grief, how old you are, and what your unique circumstances are, at some point you may decide to socialize again. This section is focused on socializing when you've lost a wife, husband, or partner. It can be particularly scary if you were married for many years, and the very thought of dating again is not something you ever considered. Your friends may try to set you up or encourage you to start socializing, while your adult children may either support you or be horrified by the prospect of Mom or Dad going out. Don't give in to anyone's pressure. Just move at your own pace and take it slowly.

Keep in mind that you may be fragile and vulnerable after losing a spouse or partner. If your spouse had a long illness, for example, your grief began when that illness started. You might be ready to get back into the social world faster than someone who lost a loved one quickly and unexpectedly. Take your time, because if you rush into this, you may not even realize that you're still grieving.

Consider taking things slowly by doing what I call *practice socializing*. If you're working, attend a social event or seminar. Don't even think about dating at this point. Just see if you have enough courage to go to an event that appeals to you, such as a seminar or community gathering, and if you can be comfortable enough to converse with people who attend. Maybe you just make small talk. It's a start.

These types of activities offer experience in meeting others. They can help you feel confident about interacting with people you didn't know.

When I felt ready to meet people after Paul died, I went online and did a search of activities for singles in my area. It took a lot of courage for me to attend several gatherings alone. I wasn't ready for online dating, so brunches, art shows, or activities that involved small groups seemed less daunting.

One event included a weekly brunch that was attended by people my age. One man seemed interesting to me, and some women I spoke with vouched for him. They said he was friendly, kind, and trustworthy. Eventually, I felt comfortable enough to accept his invitation to take me to dinner.

If meeting someone new is important to you, take your time. When you're ready, give yourself permission to consider this option. Even though your husband, wife, or partner is no longer alive, try to release the feeling that you're somehow being unfaithful to your deceased spouse or partner. This may be difficult. If it's too much of a struggle for you, then you're probably not ready.

Perhaps you may not want to get too close to someone because you're afraid of experiencing loss again. I've seen people sabotage their happiness by staying in less-than-satisfying relationships, simply because they didn't know whether they wanted it to last. They thought that if the relationship is just so-so, then it won't hurt so much when it's over. To avoid this problem, take baby steps when you consider dating. Give yourself time to know what you want and heal.

One engaging man in his eighties, Tony, who had been married for sixty years before his wife passed away, said he was ready to start meeting women. He asked me for some advice. He wanted companionship, but not a relationship. I suggested that he attend luncheons at his local senior center and to talk to some of the women who were there.

A week later, Tony told me that the women he met were friendly, but after five minutes or so, their conversations would end abruptly. I told Tony to take off his wedding ring or move it over his middle finger the next time he visited the senior center. I explained that these women thought he was still married, which is why they kept their conversations brief. Sure enough, after following my advice, Tony got a completely different reaction and said that he had great conversations with several women. He began dating one of them.

If you're ready to venture out and try meeting someone, you can still wear your wedding ring. Just move it to a place that says you're not married.

Some people prefer to use an online dating resource. This gives you the opportunity to prescreen people based on their ages, locations, interests, professions, and other criteria. People commonly meet and have short dates at a coffee shop, which provides a chance to see the person face-to-face and is the perfect venue for brief meetings.

If you're not comfortable meeting face-to-face, try Zoom. I know a variety of couples—both young and old—who met virtually during the pandemic until they were comfortable enough to meet in person. Their initial in-person dates were with masks and socially distant. Over time, they were able to spend time together just like in the old days before COVID-19.

If things work out on your virtual meeting, or in-person coffee date, you might get together at another time for a meal or a day event. If you want to break into online dating gradually, just scan the sites before you jump in. That way, you can get an idea of whom you might meet and what it could be like. A friend of mine scanned sites for months before she finally had the courage to actually meet someone.

Don't get discouraged. Some people put up old pictures, lie about their weight (I'm guilty of that), height, career, age, and so on. You may have to go on many coffee dates before you find someone compatible. Proceed cautiously and stay focused on the goal of what you want. Many couples I know have met great people they never would've encountered if they hadn't done online dating.

Travel and Day Trips Are Back

Traveling can be exciting and help people experiencing the loss of a relative or friend a chance to take a break, do something enjoyable, and heal. As we move through the pandemic, travel is starting to pick up in some locations (while slowing down in others), and people are eager to see interesting places and visit with friends and family. Where you go depends on your budget, the amount of time you have available, how the destination you want to visit is doing in terms of pandemic-related restrictions, your interests, and comfort zone.

Even just a day trip can provide the opportunity to relax and reflect on the changes in your life and plans for the future. Consider going somewhere within driving distance and packing a lunch. Perhaps you're near a city and can take advantage of museums and parks. If you have friends or family in the area that you choose to visit, you may enjoy seeing them.

Do you like solitude and want to get away some place by yourself? Maybe you need to hunker down in a quiet room with a good book and then take a walk and enjoy beautiful scenery. If your budget includes a hotel or Airbnb visit, look for places near beaches, parks, lakes, or other natural attractions. Consider going to locations you've never visited or other places that you loved but your partner didn't. Enjoy the freedom to determine your own destination.

Eddie's dad died of COVID-19 in 2020, and Eddie turned forty in 2021. Losing his father in a matter of weeks after his dad became sick, and turning a milestone age, got him thinking about what he could do that would make him feel more hopeful. He decided to plan a fortieth birthday party with his three best friends from high school. They rented a house for a few days, visited some of their favorite places, and had a great time connecting and sharing stories about their youth. It was just what Eddie needed to put a smile on his face as he thought about his future.

I have so many great memories of trips with my good friends. If you organize a trip as a group, you can split costs and have so much fun catching up. Your good friends can help you to feel better, smile, and laugh. A few of my friends from college got together, and we spent a weekend in the desert to help one of our longtime friends cope with a loss. It was like having a slumber party for grownups. We gathered again this summer, and it was just like old times. Well, not exactly. Back in our college days, the conversations focused on the men we dated and the rock concerts we attended. Instead, we spent more time trying to figure out what's next with the pandemic and what we need to do to stay healthy. Of course, we also complained about how we can no longer eat whatever we want without worrying about our weight.

If you don't have much time to travel, never underestimate the fun you can experience by taking a day trip. If you plan to drive, think about events or locales to visit. Maybe you'll drive to the city to see a play or go to a museum, or you'll experience the joy of hiking. Whether you take these jaunts by yourself or with friends, you'll be surprised at how exciting it can be to get away from your day-to-day routine and try something new.

I recently visited a museum in a nearby city and then stayed overnight at a hotel. I had forgotten how much I took for granted before COVID-19. Going to a museum, enjoying an indoor dinner with great food and real silverware, and staying at a hotel felt as exciting as traveling to Europe. It was like I was experiencing the joy of travel for the first time.

Here's a checklist of short excursions that can provide just what you need without breaking the bank, as these areas are opening up again.

- Aquariums
- Art exhibits
- Beaches
- Comedy shows
- Concerts
- Farmer's markets
- Festivals

- Gardens
- Home tours
- Lakes
- Local attractions and historic sites
- Movies
- Museums
- Parks
- Plays
- Public or miniature golf courses
- Seminars
- Spas
- Sporting events
- Wineries

If you're comfortable going on group excursions, contact your local city chamber of commerce to see what types of day trips are available. Transportation may be provided, and you'll also meet other people while you're there. Many senior centers and community centers also offer day trips. Check them out!

If you have more time and a bigger budget, consider taking a trip to a place you've never been before, and create some new memories. Traveling on your own can be fun!

Samantha decided to take a road trip to visit art galleries in Sedona, Santa Fe, and Taos, about six months after her husband died. It was something she had always wanted to do, but it never happened because her husband wasn't interested in art. Samantha was nervous because she rarely traveled alone when she was married. She spent a lot of time planning the two-week trip by searching the internet for places to visit.

Samantha discovered that the trip was just what she needed to relax. She liked the freedom of being on her own schedule, discovering new types of art, finding quaint places to eat meals, and reading or watching her favorite Netflix series at night. It gave her a chance to get away from her routine at home and simply relax.

Exploring new places with other family members or friends can be fun too. It was a lot easier to travel before the pandemic, so you may need to be more flexible if there are travel restrictions in place in certain areas. I was fortunate enough to take a long vacation with our two daughters almost two years after Paul died. I didn't want them to think of the winter holidays as another time spent without their dad. I wanted to change the dynamics of the season and create an entirely new experience for the four of us.

Our first big trip was such an exciting adventure. My younger daughter was a freshman in college, and her sister was seven years older. During this trip, I noticed that the age gap between the two of them had shrunk, and I could see that they had become closer. We visited historic sites, museums, charming cafés, and shops.

The waiter at one restaurant decided that we should sit at a table occupied by a cat, who had a bed right next to my chair. We must have looked like people who would welcome cats at the dinner table. Since we missed our cat, who was at home, the seating arrangement, although unconventional, was fine for us.

I got up the courage to see a play on my own while the girls explored other venues. This may sound like a no-brainer, but if you've never attended a play alone, you may understand why I considered this a big step toward independence. It was a turning point for me to feel comfortable enough to attend the play alone.

Paul would've been amazed that the three of us traveled for ten days in tight quarters and didn't have one argument. It was a great time of bonding.

Traveling can be comforting and eye-opening. If you have lost someone close to you and want to simply get away and try a new experience, consider a trip as an adventure and an opportunity to relax, explore, and discover new horizons.

While losing a close family member or friend is painful, you can take steps to rebuild your life and discover people and experiences to help you cope and thrive. You can't change the past, but it's possible to find positive new ways to shape your future.

LETTING THE HEALING BEGIN AND SETTING GOALS

As I've mentioned, the first year after loss can be difficult, but don't expect the loss to fade away quickly after that period. You'll have constant triggers, and coping with them should get easier over time. Everyone's circumstance is different. Here are some typical scenarios, based on Year Two and beyond after loss, and some recommendations to help you.

Knowing What to Expect

Many people join grief groups after the first year, especially if they still feel overwhelmed and want more help in working through their grief.

When Helen, who was Brenda's longtime partner, died, Brenda simply accelerated the pace of her routines and activities instead of taking time to process her grief. She worked more than ten hours a day and joined so many groups that there was little time to reflect on her loss. Just two weeks after Hel-

en's death, Brenda started a major remodeling project on her home, which was impulsive and disruptive and added to her stress level. The costs were far more than she expected.

It wasn't until Year Two, when Brenda's friends advised her to get some help, that she allowed the loss to finally sink in and joined a grief group. Through her involvement with the group, Brenda realized that she needed to reduce distractions and take the time to grieve.

Most people who put some effort into healing during the first year or so will be in better shape to set long-term goals later on. They've already done some of the hard work in processing grief. The long-term goals they set can expand on the efforts they've made during the first year. These goals may be related to their aspirations, living situation, finances, health, and relationships.

The table that follows shows you how to develop a plan for the first year. By the second year and beyond, you should be in a better position to determine which adjustments need to be made once you've gotten through the key milestones and have had a chance to deal with financial and logistical issues. You may have begun to develop some new interests, activities, and friends. The table also includes sample goals from the first year and goals and actions for the second year and beyond.

Establishing and Focusing on Long-Term Priorities

Year One Goals	Year Two and Beyond Goals	Year Two and Beyond Actions
Try to become more mentally and physically healthy.	Focus on maintaining effective mental and physical health and increase activities to support this goal.	If needed, seek counseling and join a grief group or other support program if you didn't do this during the first year. Attend a class on a topic of interest and participate in community workshops for personal growth. Exercise at least five days a week. Identify a target weight and focus on diet and nutrition to reach and maintain that goal. Make sure to get checkups, tests, and vaccines based on your doctor's recommendations.
Take control of your finances.	Implement an effective financial plan based on your goals and measure how well it's working.	Identify the amount of income you'll need each year to support your expenses. Make adjustments in a timely manner to ensure a secure future. If you like living in your home but cannot support it on one income for an extended period, consider options such as renting out a room. If you decide that it's time to relocate and downsize or to relocate to be closer to family, friends, or employment opportunities, do your research and set a feasible target date to move.

157

Year One Goals	Year Two and Beyond Goals	Year Two and Beyond Actions
Take control of your finances (cont.).	Implement an effective financial plan based on your goals and measure how well it's working (cont.).	If you're not working but need additional income, look into full-time or part-time employment. If you have a business network, seek the help of people you know. If not, begin to search online for opportunities and explore community resources that can help you. If you want to learn a new skill or start a job in an area where you lack expertise, consider doing volunteer work in that field to help build up your experience. If you have disabilities or need public assistance, contact your local city government offices to find out what resources are available to you. Update your estate plan.
Visit with friends and family more often when it's practical. Some visits may need to be virtual.	Visit with friends and family more often in person when it's practical.	Identify a target number of days per month or quarter that you will visit with friends and family and contact them to arrange visits. Join a community group from your place of worship or other organization.
If you have a job, try not to take on more work than you can handle.	Consider expanding your career opportunities if you're working and your current position isn't meeting your objectives.	If your current position isn't providing the income, benefits, flexibility, or challenge that you expected, set a target date for looking into your options. This could be applying for other jobs in your company, getting training to learn a new skill, or looking at outside opportunities. It may mean going from full-time to part-time, or even branching out on your own as a freelancer.

Year One Goals	Year Two and Beyond Goals	Year Two and Beyond Actions
Take a music class, even if it's only available virtually.	Take a music class and join a local choir. Some choirs perform virtually. Consider pursuing other hobbies.	Continue singing in the choir and taking classes, as desired. If you have other hobbies you want to pursue, then identify what they are and set a date when you will be ready to get involved.
Identify what makes you happy and gives you something to look forward to doing.	Implement a plan to make these activities a reality and start to explore some of them.	The first year after a loss can be chaotic and cause you to be conflicted or confused. You may have tried different things to make you happy, only to discover that they were just Band-Aid solutions to satisfy immediate cravings for comfort. By now, you should be able to think more clearly about what changes you need to make on your path to happiness. Set some clear long-term goals and develop and implement a plan to reach them.
Take some day trips with a friend or relative.	Put a travel plan into action. If you need to save extra money to travel, identify what's needed and how you plan to make that happen.	Identify places you'd like to visit. Plan a trip based on your interests, budget, comfort zone, and then take it.
	New goal: Think about what you might like to do as a volunteer.	Volunteer to participate in a local charity. Specifically identify a cause or causes that are important to you. Determine how many hours you can contribute to that organization each month, and set a date when you can join that group as a volunteer.

Once you've developed these long-term goals, take out a calendar (I prefer one that has plenty of space for each day so that I can add notes), set target dates, and determine what you're going to do throughout the year to reach these goals. Objectives that go into the following year can be carried over in a separate calendar. Although you might not be able to accomplish everything, do what's reasonable. Just keep in mind that you can't reach your destination without a map. Let your calendar be your map.

Stephen Covey, the author of *The Seven Habits of Highly Effective People*, once said, "Begin with the end in mind." Take that approach. By understanding your priorities and setting incremental goals, you can expedite healing and experience happiness and growth.

8

Understanding Different Types of Losses

People will adjust to the COVID-19 era differently based on their relationship with the person who died and their own unique situations. Here are some examples to consider.

Loss of Husband, Wife, or Partner

At some point after your loss, you may consider dating or entering into a new relationship. The examples described in this section happened before the pandemic, but they are still relevant today. What you're looking for at your present stage of life might be different from what you wanted when you were with the person you're grieving. Some people I know who lost their spouses or partners were happy to have friendships with companions. They wanted someone who could join them at events, restaurants, parties, and other activities.

Other widows I've known were married a long time to their husbands, and over the years, their relationships had soured due to issues like infidelity, alcoholism, or just by growing apart. These women still loved their late husbands but wanted to make sure that they didn't repeat mistakes of the past in any future relationship.

We all have our routines and priorities, and they become more ingrained as we age. Set your expectations based on what's most important to you and how much you're willing to compromise. A widow or widower may have an enjoyable, steady relationship with someone, but choose not to live with that person because of conflicting values, priorities, or other circumstances. They might like to live alone for a while.

Some people decide to pursue their passions—such as art, music, reading, gardening, writing, or sports—rather than get involved in a new relationship. They might also prefer to expand their network of friends to provide a more satisfying social structure and stave off loneliness.

How Losing a Spouse or Partner Affects Their Children

Losing someone when you're in your twenties or thirties is devastating, but due to potential longevity, people in this age group may, in time, be more likely to remarry or establish a long-term partnership than someone much older.

If they have a child or children, they may yearn to have a suitable father or mother figure enter their lives at some point. If they don't have children, this might be an opportunity to have the family they always wanted. Of course, entering into a new relationship, especially when it involves blending families, takes effort, understanding, and patience. Many people, however, are willing to take that leap to find love and happiness again.

Fred married his college sweetheart, Sheryl, when he was twenty-nine. They built a wonderful life together, moved around the country, and had exciting jobs. After they'd been married for about four years, they decided to have children. Sheryl wasn't able to conceive because she had ovarian cysts. After additional testing, they discovered that she had ovarian cancer.

During the first year of Sheryl's diagnosis, Fred began the grieving process and spent considerable time in denial. He did everything he could to support her, keep her comfortable, and try to help her heal. He moved on to acceptance when he realized that the surgery and chemo would no longer help and that she wasn't going to live.

Sheryl fought the battle with cancer for three years with chemotherapy and surgery, but she couldn't win. Near the end, hospice provided comfort care for her in their home, with Fred by her side. When she passed, Fred felt a deep loss, but he also was relieved that she would no longer suffer.

Fred accepted that his life would start on a new path and that at age thirty-nine, he still had many years ahead of him. He wasn't interested in attending grief groups. His mom and close friend were with Fred when Sheryl passed, but he wanted to keep his grief personal and deal with it on his own terms and at his own pace. He had done all that he could to help Sheryl, so Fred didn't experience survivor's guilt, which happens to many people.

Fred became very involved in his work as an engineer to help pass the time, pay the bills, and provide the much-needed structure in his life. After several months, he decided that he was ready to socialize and went to a community event for singles. There, he met a woman who said she'd like to set up Fred on a blind date with her close friend, Wendy. (Keep in mind that this was how many people met each other before there were personal ads and online dating services.)

Fred never expected to begin a new relationship — he wasn't looking for one — but when he met Wendy, he was drawn to her for many reasons. Wendy was attractive, compassionate, honest, interesting, and intelligent.

Fred and Wendy have been happily married for many years. He has no regrets about meeting her soon after Sheryl died, and had no desire to date anyone else before settling down. Fred had married Sheryl when he was thirty and had dated enough women before meeting Sheryl that he knew what he wanted in a partner. Wendy met all of his expectations and more. He also got along well with Wendy's young daughter. Fred and Wendy had a son a few years after they were married. Fred's new path brought him happiness, healing, and a family.

It's increasingly possible that some of your grown children may be living with you. More adult children have moved back home with their parents due to the pandemic. Maybe they lost their jobs and needed a place to live. Or they needed you to help with day care. Perhaps they even moved in to help you if you have medical issues.

So not only are you dealing with your own loss, but you also have to recognize what your children are going through and give them the support they need. Even if your children are grown and out of the house, they likely will need to grapple with their loss and may not understand the challenges you face because they're focused on their own suffering.

After her husband died of a sudden heart attack, Tina threw herself into her work. Meanwhile, her son, Eric, had problems in school, and his grades dropped dramatically. He spent far too much time online, began to withdraw from his friends, and started drinking alcohol.

Tina was overwhelmed. The loss of her husband and shock of his sudden death caused her great anxiety. She had trouble sleeping at night and was worried about how she could possibly keep her business going, pay the bills, and deal with her loneliness.

It wasn't until she got into a car accident that she realized she needed to get help. Tina had been distracted, didn't notice a red light, and crashed into the car in front of her. Fortunately, no one was injured in the accident, but it was just one more stress factor at a time when her coping skills were eroding.

Tina signed up for one-on-one grief support at her local hospice. By attending that program, she realized that she was not alone. Tina discovered that she needed a plan to understand how the loss affected her so that she could put her life back together successfully and steer Eric in the right direction. With the help of a grief counselor, Tina learned how to release the guilt of not being able to save her husband's life.

Loss of Spouse and Partner When You're a Senior

Seniors today often lead a lifestyle that may be more active and healthier than the lifestyle that their parents experienced. For example, their parents were raised at a time when smoking was not considered a health hazard. Many health breakthroughs that weren't available to their parents have helped them to expand their longevity and quality of life. With a good diet, exercise, and self-care, you're more likely to live longer and feel younger. I've heard people say that seventy is the "new" fifty. That sounds good to me!

One of the advantages of reaching Medicare age is that you likely have a better understanding of who you are and what you want at this point in your life. You may have already accomplished goals that you established earlier, whether it's career objectives, owning a home, spending time with your friends or adult children and grandchildren (if you have them), focusing on volunteer work or other priorities that really matter. Having this insight about your own interests and values can enable you to be more selective as you determine what you want to do. If you're seeking another relationship, you could more likely know what to look for at this time in your life. Here's an example of getting outside your comfort zone:

Donna and her husband, Steve, got married when they were in their late thirties. He was an accountant, and she taught third grade. They didn't have children, but they both enjoyed an active social life with friends and often hiked together on the weekends. When Steve was sixty-four, he died from complications after a skiing accident when he and Donna were on vacation. Donna wasn't a skier, so she wasn't present when the accident happened.

Steve was in the hospital for several days before he developed a severe infection that quickly caused his body to shut down. For several months after his death, Donna just wanted to stay at home. Steve died six months after Donna had retired from teaching, so not only did she lose her husband, but she also had just recently ended her career. She stopped exercising and lost her appetite. She struggled with sleep and rarely answered the phone or looked at her mail. Donna had a large circle of friends but only a small group of family members that included two cousins, a sister-in-law, and a niece, all of whom lived three thousand miles away.

About three months after Steve died, Donna decided that she was ready to seek help. She signed up for a grief group at her local hospice and began attending church on Sundays. The grief group provided much-needed structure to her life, which included a place she had to be once a week, along with people who would understand her loss and help her to complete incremental goals. Her Sunday visits to church also gave Donna an opportunity to be around people in a healing environment.

When Steve died, several of Donna's close friends tried to reach out to her. But Donna wasn't ready to share her loss with them. After attending several grief group sessions and church visits, she finally realized that if she was going to heal, she had to accept the help and companionship of her friends. Donna needed to come to terms with what she wanted and planned to do for this phase of her life. Steve didn't get the chance to live another twenty or thirty years with her. She realized that time was limited, and she owed it to him — and herself — to make the most out of life.

Donna decided that she needed to get out more and give herself permission to experience joy again. She'd visit with friends, exercise regularly, take a pottery class, and work part-time as a substitute teacher. Getting back into the workplace, even just two days a week, gave Donna a sense of purpose and provided extra income to supplement her retirement. Donna knew that she would now be responsible for her financial future on her own. Going back to work helped address that challenge.

Once Donna got through the financial hurdles and was back into a routine, she thought about what it would be like to have a companion. She had to convince herself that she wasn't replacing Steve — he was a unique person, and she would always hold his memories in her heart. She considered the possibility that there was someone else out there she would enjoy spending time with and getting to know.

When you're in your eighties and beyond, and you lose your spouse or partner, you may feel how lucky you are to have enjoyed each other for so long. That's looking at the situation from a positive perspective. On the other hand, if you've spent most of your life with your spouse or partner, it's difficult to imagine life without this person.

Many of the older seniors I've met married their spouses when they were in their late teens or early twenties. Some of the women of that generation never worked outside the home. They raised their families and took care of the meals and social activities, but often delegated handling the finances to their husbands. Suddenly, they were faced with making financial decisions that were new to them at a time in their lives when they felt particularly vulnerable. Their husbands were frequently the ones who took care of home repairs, carried out the trash, and so on.

They've tended to handle their loss better if they had a good support system of friends, family, or religious community. Many of them relied on their adult children to help them as they navigated their way through the grief process and gradually assumed some of the tasks handled by their husbands. Keep in mind that these women, like men, also had to deal with their own health issues, like problems with mobility, hearing, and vision, which tend to compound as you get older. These problems happened to them at the same time they had to cope with the loss of their loved ones.

Men in their eighties and beyond generally took on the role of the key financial provider, but were less likely to cook, do laundry, clean up, and plan social activities. They also were less likely to seek outside help, such as attending grief groups or seeing therapists. Many of them relied on their families, when possible, to provide much-needed support.

My father had no idea how to cook. When he was in his fifties, even the microwave was a challenge to him. His generation was different from mine (baby boomers), Gen X, and younger generations, who are much more likely to share household responsibilities.

People who lose their loved ones in their eighties and beyond likely have to take on new roles and responsibilities that once were delegated to their spouses or partners. They're also more likely to have other losses that are not as often experienced by prior generations. Their friends may have passed away. Or they had to stop driving, which can represent a loss of independence. They may resent having to rely on their children for help or to be unable to obtain the help they need. They could have health issues that affect their mobility and quality of life.

What's especially difficult is having to leave their familiar homes because the level of upkeep is too much to handle alone. They may also have to move to a senior facility or relocate and leave their existing social network behind to be closer to family members.

Rachel was eighty-two when her husband, Adam, died of complications from Alzheimer's. She and Adam had raised three daughters, who all lived two thousand miles away. Rachel and Adam retired in their late sixties and enjoyed the nightlife of Chicago and the activities in the city.

By the time Adam was seventy-eight, he started experiencing memory loss. He became quiet when they socialized, withdrew from activities, and was under a doctor's care. Rachel cut back on social events but tried to make sure that she and Adam went out for meals occasionally and took walks together. One night he left the house in his bathrobe, wandered through the neighborhood and couldn't remember where he lived. What made matters worse was that he exited through a window, not a door.

After that incident, Rachel met with her doctor and decided to put Adam in a memory care facility, where he would be safe. Rachel was dealing with her own health issues — diabetes and hypertension — but tried to keep those conditions under control and focus on Adam. It was painful to see the man who was once so vital and sharp lose the ability to communicate effectively and process information. Still, she visited him each day and cherished the times when he would smile or utter something that sparked a pleasant memory. When he passed, Rachel missed him dearly, but she also felt a sense of relief because she knew that Adam hadn't wanted to live that way.

The medical costs for Adam's care took a huge chunk out of what had once been a large retirement fund. Rachel had to cope with the loss and make major financial decisions. She sold her home and most of her belongings, other than the items that her daughters wanted to keep, and moved to Florida to be near them and her grandchildren. It was difficult for Rachel to leave her friends and the house that she loved when she moved away from Chicago.

Her oldest daughter, Sarah, invited Rachel to live with their family. Rachel declined because she liked being independent. So she moved into a one-bedroom apartment in a senior-living facility near Sarah's family.

Even though it was a big change and not the way she had ever intended to spend her final years, Rachel established goals for her new life. She made it a point to meet new people at her senior home, which had more than one hundred residents. Instead of eating meals alone in her apartment, for example, she went to the cafeteria for lunch and dinner. The facility had bus trips to movies, plays, museums, and other activities that Rachel attended.

Over time, she met several new friends who joined her for meals and some of the events. She didn't let her impaired mobility keep her from enjoying these activities. She got around by using a walker, and her hearing aids made it possible to join in conversations without feeling that she was missing out.

Rachel was surprised at how easy it was to meet people. She also volunteered to participate in a weekly cooking program, in which some residents at her senior center prepared meals for a local homeless shelter. She loved to cook and found a new sense of accomplishment in being able to provide a service to her new community.

Rachel attended religious services weekly with her daughter and visited her grandchildren at least once or twice a week. While she missed Adam terribly, Rachel was comforted by knowing that she could spend more time with her family now that she had relocated. Rachel shared stories about Adam with her children and grandchildren and kept his memory alive. Over time, by thinking about everything that made their relationship so special and talking about the good times, the images of Adam during his illness faded away and were replaced with happy memories.

Loss of Sibling

When you lose a brother or sister, your relationship with your parents, if one or both of them are still alive, changes. Depending on the age of your sibling who died, your own age, and the number of children in your family, your role in the family structure changes. For example, if your father passed away years ago and your only brother, who is younger than you, just died unexpectedly, life gets very complicated. You'll have to address a variety of challenges before becoming "whole" again.

This can lead to conflicting feelings. Your mom may depend on you more than ever before. Even though you want to help her, it can put an increased demand on you at a time when you're struggling to keep your job and your relationship with your partner.

Here's why it's important to take the time to identify your priorities. If this means that you need to find someone to take over some of the responsibilities of helping your mom, look into resources that might be available. If you live a significant distance from her, try to set up regular calls several times a week and schedule periodic visits, whether it's once a month, every few months, or longer. There may be community services available to handle transportation, meal delivery, and so forth.

Guilt is also a big concern. Perhaps you and your brother experienced typical sibling rivalry, and now you feel tremendously guilty for the times that you could've tried to be more patient with him and spend more time together. You thought you'd have many years ahead where you could make up for lost time, but now it's gone. This is a normal response to grief. Try to focus on the things that went well in your relationship. Go easy on yourself.

If, on the other hand, you and your brother were very close and saw each other frequently, losing him creates a tremendous hole that you feel you won't be able to escape. You miss him terribly. Try some of the healing exercises discussed in this book, such as journaling, writing a letter to your brother, creating artwork, or planting something in a garden to remember him. Seek out others in a grief group who've been through a similar situation.

Survivor's guilt also kicks in if your parents treated you as their favorite child and your brother didn't get the same opportunities they offered to you. Survivor's guilt is common. Just accept that what you're feeling is normal. You can't change what happened in the past, and each family has its own dynamic. Therapy and grief support can be very helpful as you work through these issues.

You can become frustrated because you feel obligated to move hundreds of miles to be closer to your mom, but you don't want to do this. It could be very disruptive to your life. That's why it's important to be true to yourself. If you leave your community and disrupt your life out of obligation, it could exacerbate your feelings of loss.

You and your mom might have never been close, and having to make all these adjustments is more than you can handle. Or you and your mom were so close that you're ready to change your whole life just to help her—even if it means risking your relationship with your partner by relocating and hurts your career. That's why you need to understand your limits and priorities and try not to take on responsibilities that are beyond your capabilities. There are ways that you can help your mom without jeopardizing your other relationships and career.

If you follow the best practices I've discussed in the book and get help to work through these challenges and issues that are unique to you, then you'll be in a better position to assess what actions you need or want to take to help your mother and yourself through this difficult time.

Loss of Child or Grandchild

Children are expected to outlive their parents and grandparents. It's the natural order of things and an assumption that we make. So when a child dies, this loss is unimaginable. The stress caused by losing a child is the reason why so many couples divorce after this happens. Whether that loss is by an illness, a miscarriage, an accident, death by suicide, or other tragic cause, it can be simply devastating. Here are some of the emotions that you might be experiencing if you've lost a child and how to cope with them.

If the child was killed in a car accident and you were driving, it's difficult to let go of the guilt you might feel—even if you drove safely and got hit by a drunk driver. Or if the child died of an illness, you may fret that you didn't do enough to keep her well. If you lost a baby due to miscarriage, you may blame yourself, even though it's simply not your fault.

The burden of losing a child can be unbearable, and the pandemic exacerbates this situation. If you don't address the pain you're feeling and work through it, it will hover in the background, taking its toll.

It could be more difficult for parents and grandparents to do tasks that were once so easy. You may not feel like returning to work if you have a job. If this loss happened during certain periods in the pandemic, you might not have been able to have visitors who could help you work through the loss, or even drop by and comfort you. You and the other parent of this child might have drifted apart because you're both suffering so much.

Talk about your child with others and get professional help. The same advice applies to the grandparents and others, who are also feeling the pain of this loss. Try to cut back on responsibilities that are overwhelming and take the time to grieve. If you're still working, it might even be helpful to take a leave from work or cut back on your hours if possible while you process this loss.

Have some healing rituals. Keep a picture of your child with you, look at it before you go to bed, and say something out loud or write down what you'd want that child to hear. Cry when you want to. Don't be afraid to express your feelings.

Grief can make you confused and distracted, so don't be surprised if you get sudden memory lapses, find it difficult to complete a task that once was so easy, start crying for no reason, or seem disinterested in engaging with people. Many people struggle with making decisions after loss. These feelings are common, but with professional help, you can find ways to adjust to the new normal.

The loss of a child affects not only you, but other family members and friends. They're also suffering and experiencing some of the pain that you're going through. Try to be patient with yourself and with them.

Loss of a Parent, Stepparent, or Grandparent

Many people have lost their parents, stepparents, or grandparents during the pandemic and are still grappling with the aftermath, whether it was caused by COVID-19, another illness, an accident, or even social isolation. When your parent dies, your role changes. If it's the second parent to die, you suddenly become an orphan. It doesn't matter if that person was over one hundred years old. You've known your parent or grandparent all your life, so it can be difficult to imagine being without them.

Remind yourself that it will take considerable time to work through this loss. Share memories of this person with friends and family members. Find a special place in your home to commemorate them. When you're feeling particularly sad and missing them, remind yourself about why you were so grateful to have them in your life.

Stepparents often have close relationships with their spouse's or partner's children, and losing them can be very much like losing a parent, particularly if they've been in your life for many years. Recognize that this could be a significant loss, and apply the same techniques discussed in this book to help you work through your emotions, such as journaling, signing up for music or art therapy, connecting with people who help fill that void (such as a favorite aunt or uncle), and engaging with professionals or clergy experienced in helping people cope with these circumstances.

Getting professional help is particularly important when a child loses a parent. Children may freeze or withdraw and be unable to talk about their feelings of loss. It's more than they can process. Programs such as art therapy that encourage creative expression, music therapy, retreats with other children who have lost a parent, and one-on-one sessions give children an opportunity to share their emotions, be heard, and supported.

***

Maggie, a nurse who lived with her parents, worked closely with COVID-19 patients in a hospital. She donned her protective clothing at work and often worked long shifts. She'd immediately take a shower each day after returning home, just because it made her extra safe at a time when we were trying to understand how COVID-19 was spread.

One night Maggie's mother, Fiona, got a high fever, lost her sense of smell and taste, and ultimately tested positive. Fiona was rushed to the hospital but had underlying health conditions that made her more vulnerable, and she died within ten days.

Maggie, who was asymptomatic, blamed herself for causing her mother's death and was deeply depressed. She thought about all the lives she had saved and was haunted by the fact that it was own mother who had died. It was only through therapy and grief support sessions that Maggie eventually was able to forgive herself. She was just doing her job. Fiona had always been proud of Maggie for her commitment to helping people. Maggie held on to that memory, as it helped her to cope with the loss of her mother.

Loss of a Friend

Losing a close friend can be like losing a family member, particularly if that friend has been in your life for so many years. Some of the exercises discussed earlier, such as writing a letter to your friend describing your feelings, can be helpful. Then follow up with a letter from your friend to you responding to those emotions.

Rituals or activities that you would do to commemorate a family member might be similar to the ones for a friend — create a memory box, journal, celebrate your friend's birthday by eating her favorite food, put a post in her memory on social media, and so on.

When a good friend of mine died of cancer, I would take a walk periodically in a place we used to go and just think about her. I'd quietly talk to myself and tell her what's going in my life, how much I miss her, and that our friendship meant so much to me.

Some people find it healing to stay in touch with others who knew your friend and share memories of that person. If your friend had children, try to connect with them—whether it involves visiting, calling, texting, or liking and commenting on their posts on social media about their parent. You can make a difference in their lives by helping keep the memory of their mom or dad alive.

Loss of Aunts, Uncles, In-Laws, Nieces, Nephews, and Cousins, and Other Relatives

You may have some favorite relatives who were an important part of your life. You miss them. This is why it's particularly important for families to come together and share memories. Bring out photos of these people and tell stories with other family members about what these relatives meant to you and what makes them so special.

Perhaps you were close to your aunt or uncle. My uncle lived thirty-plus years longer than my dad, and he was one of the father figures in my life. Although he was three thousand miles away, we stayed connected over the years and I'd visit with him periodically. When he died, it was comforting to see my cousin and his family and stay in touch with other relatives who shared fond memories of him. Sometimes I reach out to my uncle's family with a comment or "like" on Facebook. While I don't spend much time doing my own posts on social media, I think it's a convenient way to keep up with what's happening with people who are important to you.

Many cousins grew up together like siblings. Mothers-in-law or fathers-in-law were like parents. Brothers-in-law and sisters-in-law became as close as siblings. You may think of your stepchildren, nieces, and nephews the same as your children or as the children you never had. When you grieve for them, the steps you take to heal can be based on how close they were to you.

9

FINDING HAPPINESS AGAIN

Love can take many forms, whether it's finding a new relationship or enjoying time with friends and family. It can be discovering a new hobby, volunteer activity, or career based on your passion. The conundrum is that people may know what they *don't* want, but they don't always know what they *do* want.

If you lost a spouse or partner and began dating someone who seems special, here are some things to keep in mind. It's a lot easier to have a relationship with someone you don't have to try to change. If you have differences, determine whether they are workable. For example, if you're a staunch conservative, and this person is a progressive liberal, consider avoiding discussing politics to keep your relationship on track. If you're super-organized and this individual is sloppy, it doesn't have to be a deal breaker. You can offer to take over certain organizational functions, like putting dishes away after you remove them from the dishwasher or planning activities.

You might also wonder whether at some point you can love someone deeply again after you lose your loved one. I can tell you from my own experience—and from many people who have loved and lost—that yes, you can. It doesn't take away from what you had before. It's a way to build on who you are now. Many years after Paul died, I met a wonderful man, Jack. We got married, and I'm very happy and grateful to share my life with him.

Loving a New Career or Fulfilling Activity

Many people are satisfied with pursuing other activities as they begin to rebuild their lives after loss. After all, spending a year or more in a lockdown state likely left you with some free time to help sort out your own identity, priorities, and passions — things you may want to pursue. Here's a pre-pandemic example of career change after loss that is still quite valid today.

Tonya had always enjoyed writing, but she chose a career as a software developer because it seemed like a practical and lucrative field. She took some creative writing and poetry classes in high school and college and considered them a pleasant break from the math and science courses that her parents pressured her to pursue. She never fully enjoyed her job, which was her career up until she took a leave of absence at age sixty-five, after the death of her husband. Because working in the tech industry was lucrative, and Tonya had skills that were in demand, she had managed to accumulate sizable savings for her retirement.

After José died, Tonya didn't feel like returning to her unrelenting job that offered many perks. It took every last bit of energy she had, between training new staff members, traveling, commuting, and doing her own coding. Not only that, but her co-workers were all younger than her children. She wasn't motivated to participate in the after-hours social activities sponsored by her employer. Once she became eligible for Medicare, Tonya didn't have the financial pressure of worrying about health insurance. With these conditions in mind, Tonya was ready for a change.

Tonya loved pets and wanted to write books about how to raise and train animals and eventually get work experience as an animal trainer. She fostered a variety of dogs as a hobby. She was ready to make a difference in a field that combined her desire to write with her interest in helping people take better care of their pets.

Tonya began her career incrementally by joining a Meetup group of local writers and researching dog-training best practices. She took a weekend workshop on how to develop and self-publish a book and became more active in her local community. She also took classes in animal training and volunteered to walk dogs for people with mobility disabilities, such as individuals who were recovering from injuries. It was important for her to create a structure where she'd have regular meetings, classes, and volunteer work, in addition to blocking out time to do her writing.

Of course, Tonya missed José tremendously, but she was ready to transform as she entered this new chapter in her life. It was the right time for her to make a change. The dramatic shift in her career — from software developer/ manager to writer/animal trainer/volunteer — provided the creative satisfaction that she yearned for but had repressed for many years. Instead of commuting an average of three hours a day, she now had time to exercise and visit with friends.

As she became more involved in her multiple business activities, she expanded her social network. Tonya had lost the love of her life, but she blossomed in ways that were satisfying and that enabled her to find happiness.

Enjoying the Company of Family and Friends

Many people have found that spending more time with their relatives and friends helps them stay focused and happy. One widower I know watches his grandchildren after school each day. His close relationship with them is rewarding for him and the grandchildren. While he has also developed many friendships with women and men in his community, he continues to make the grandkids his number-one priority.

After loss, some adults may look to create stronger ties with their siblings, even if they weren't close as children.

Amy and Julie lived three thousand miles apart, and they had different occupations and interests. Julie lived in New York City, was divorced, and worked as a waitress in Manhattan. Amy was a psychologist and was married to a doctor, William.

William died suddenly of an infection after heart surgery, about two months after Amy and Julie's mother passed away from cancer. At that time, Amy was forty-eight. Their father had died ten years earlier, and while both women felt a significant loss after losing both of their parents, they hadn't been particularly close with their mother.

While they were growing up, the two sisters, who were about fourteen years apart, had separate social circles and interests. Amy, the older sister, saw Julie, at most, once a year during annual family gatherings after Amy left home to go to college and graduate school. They got along okay with each other, but didn't have much in common and drifted apart. Neither had any children.

When Amy's husband died, Amy's loss was compounded by the death of her mother. Amy mourned her husband and the relationship that she'd wanted to have with her mom, but never nurtured. She had no cousins, parents, aunts, uncles, children, nieces, or nephews. Amy felt abandoned and distraught and began to realize that Julie must have experienced some of the same emotions when she divorced Hank.

Amy gradually became aware that Julie was her connection to the past, and she wanted to explore that relationship further and try to improve it. She invited Julie to go with her on a trip to Alaska. The sisters traveled together and tried to make up for lost time. In the past, Amy had been too quick to judge Julie for having less-ambitious career goals. Now she recognized that Julie had dropped out of college to help their father, who was chronically ill. Julie worked as a waitress part-time so that she could assist the family. When caring for the family became too intense for Julie's husband, he simply left her.

Meanwhile, Julie resented the fact that Amy had the opportunity to go to college and pursue a prestigious career, an option that wasn't available to Julie because of her obligations to her parents.

On their trip, Julie discovered that although her sister wasn't physically present to take care of their parents, Amy worked overtime to send her mother money to support the family. As they shared their perspectives, each sister became more aware of the other's motivations, and they became more sympathetic and supportive of each other.

One of the biggest challenges that you'll face after losing your loved one is coping with loneliness. Your close relatives may live far away. You might have health limitations that affect your ability to engage in activities that once brought you joy, like hiking, swimming, cycling, or painting.

What can you do to feel fulfilled and connected again? Consider building on your existing friendships and reaching out to meet new people. After all, many people are in a similar situation to yours, and they have the same needs for friendship. This is why it's important to feel like part of a community, and you can make that happen by living in the place that best fits your needs.

If you have children, think about what it was like when you were raising a family and the choices you made. For example, Paul and I relocated to Santa Cruz County from Los Angeles when my youngest daughter was in the fourth grade. We wanted to find a new home in a community with good schools and other families raising children.

My neighborhood friends were like my family, and that's the same type of friendship you can develop, even later in life. They can be people from your place of worship who gather for group activities. Or they can be people who regularly attend your exercise class. If you live in a senior community, you may be surrounded by people in a situation similar to yours. This can provide opportunities to participate in local activities, meet for coffee or tea, take a class, walk together, and much more. These friends can give you something to look forward to each day.

In addition to the new people you can meet, you may have long-term friends who have played an important role in your life. They also may have lost someone close to them. Continue to cultivate the relationships with those people who give you joy. They are your connection with the past and can play an important role in the future. Learning to love again can mean different things to each individual.

CONCLUSION

When you first lose someone close to you, particularly during the COVID-19 era and beyond, it may be difficult to think that you'll ever be able to experience joy again. Dealing with the loss, especially if it was unexpected, and at such a challenging time, can be overwhelming. Handling even the most basic daily activities can seem impossible. By carefully working through your grief, getting help when you need it, and setting incrementally achievable goals, you can rebuild your life and find happiness again.

You don't have to heal alone. Contact your local hospice and sign up for one-on-one sessions or a grief support group, even if the group meets virtually. It's important to talk about your emotions and challenges as you work your way through loss. Grief groups, for example, offer a safe, nonjudgmental, supportive environment for sharing and healing.

Many hospices offer sessions for coping with all types of losses and have a variety of programs available. Some hospices make these services available to everyone in their community and not just families of hospice patients. If you have children who are grieving, consider getting them help as well. There are specialized programs available to children, including camping, art therapy, and other activities.

Follow the healing approach that works best for you. Depending on your situation, you may decide to see a therapist or someone to provide spiritual assistance. There is no standard time frame for being over grief, and the pandemic has certainly made the healing process much more challenging, but you can rediscover yourself and experience exciting opportunities you may have never imagined. This can include starting a new career, following a creative passion, doing volunteer work that gives you satisfaction, building new friendships and relationships, and becoming closer to the people who are important to you. It's all up to you.

ACKNOWLEDGMENTS

I'd like to thank my entire family and friends for the love and support they have given me throughout the years. I am so grateful to have them all in my life, and it has been a blessing welcoming each new family member over time — grandchildren, spouses, and more. My journey with my late husband Paul was what inspired me to become involved with hospice and write books, including this one, to help people work through their grief and find hope.

My husband Jack encouraged me to write this book, and I thank him for his patience while I spent many nights discussing endless details about the content and how it relates to the challenges that people are facing today.

Many thanks to Denise Kalm, my friend and the coauthor of our book, *Tech Grief — Survive and Thrive Through Career Losses*, who painstakingly reviewed the first draft of this book and gave me extremely helpful feedback. I'd also like to thank all the people who helped me with my second book, *After Loss — Hope for Widows, Widowers, and Partners*. Their guidance has also shaped this book about loss during a pandemic.

I'd like to recognize the team at Hospice of Santa Cruz County for all that they do to continue to support people with compassion, dignity, and exceptional care. Special recognition also goes to the people who shared their stories with me and for everyone else involved in making this book possible.

ABOUT THE AUTHOR

 Linda Donovan is an award-winning author, grief support advocate, and marketing consultant for technology companies. Her work has appeared in books, blogs, newspapers, magazines, and popular online publications.

Linda has been leading grief support groups for Hospice of Santa Cruz County for more than a decade. She became involved with her local hospice after experiencing how the team provided so much assistance to her family before and after the death of her late husband, Paul.

Linda is the co-author of *Tech Grief: Survive and Thrive Through Career Losses*, which won a Writer's Digest Award, and the author of *After Loss: Hope for Widows, Widowers and Partners*. She has taught writing courses at three universities, and has been a featured speaker at book clubs, hospice community gatherings and webinars, as well as technology conferences.

Website: lindadonovanbooks.com

BOOK CLUB TOPICS FOR DISCUSSION

1. What are a few ways that you can help someone who is grieving?

2. Describe some of the additional challenges people face in dealing with loss that happened during the pandemic and how they can address those challenges.

3. Discuss different ways to stay connected with people when it's no longer possible to gather in person.

4. Some people experience survivor's guilt. How can you cope with that challenge and work through it?

5. Describe how the loss of the person close to you has changed your role and responsibilities, and how that impacts you.

6. What self-care mean to you?

7. Describe some rituals that can help you work through your grief.

8. What do you plan to do to avoid feeling isolated?

9. What steps can you take to set boundaries with people so that you don't take on more than you can handle?

10. How has losing someone changed your perspective on what's most important to you?

11. Why do you think it's so difficult for some people to talk about their grief?

12. What goals will you set for yourself over the next year?

13. Describe how you felt after you completed the grief timeline exercise.

14. If you decide to write a letter to the person who died, what would you want to tell them?

15. What did you learn about how different types of losses impact people?

Made in the USA
Monee, IL
29 April 2022

95237301R00115